SCHOOLS

When education activists in New York, Chicago, and other urban school districts in the 1980s began the small-schools movement, they envisioned a new kind of public school system that was fair and equitable and that encouraged new relationships between teachers and students. When that movement for school reform ran head-on into the neo-conservative takeover of the Department of Education and its No Child Left Behind strategy for school change, a new model of federal power bent on the erosion of public space and the privatization of public schooling emerged. Michael and Susan Klonsky, educators who were among the early leaders of the small-schools movement, tell the story of how a once-promising model of creating new small and charter schools has been used by the neocons to reproduce many of the old inequities. *Small Schools: Public School Reform Meets the Ownership Society* is the engaging story of what happens when the small-schools movement meets the Ownership Society.

Michael Klonsky Ph.D. is a professor of education and director of the Center for Innovative Schools.

Susan Klonsky is Director of Development, Small Schools Workshop.

Positions: Education, Politics, and Culture

Edited by Kenneth J. Saltman, DePaul University, and Ron Scapp, College of Mount St. Vincent

SMALL
SCHOOLS

PUBLIC SCHOOL
REFORM MEETS
THE OWNERSHIP SOCIETY

MICHAEL KLONSKY
AND
SUSAN KLONSKY

Routledge
Taylor & Francis Group

NEW YORK AND LONDON

First published 2008
by Routledge
270 Madison Ave, New York, NY 10016

Simultaneously published in the UK
by Routledge
2 Park Square, Milton Park, Abingdon, Oxon OX14 4RN

Routledge is an imprint of the Taylor & Francis Group, an informa business

© 2008 Routledge, Taylor and Francis

Typeset in Minion by
HWA Text and Data Management, Tunbridge Wells
Printed and bound in the United States of America on acid-free paper by
Walsworth Publishing Company, Marceline, MO

Library of Congress Cataloging in Publication Data
Klonsky, Michael.
Small schools : public school reform meets the ownership society / Michael Klonsky
and Susan Klonsky.
p. cm. – (Positions : education, politics, and culture)
Includes bibliographical references and index.
1. Small schools–United States. 2. School size–United States. 3. Public schools–United
States. I. Klonsky, Susan. II. Title.
LB3012.5.K56 2008
371.00973–dc22   2007035976

ISBN10: 0–415–96122–X (hbk)
ISBN10: 0–415–96123–8 (pbk)
ISBN10: 0–203–93185–8 (ebk)

ISBN13: 978–0–415–96122–6 (hbk)
ISBN13: 978–0–415–96123–3 (pbk)
ISBN13: 978–0–203–93185–1 (ebk)

Contents

Positions is a series interrogating the intersections of education, politics, and culture. Books in the series are short, polemical, and accessibly written, merging rigorous scholarship with politically engaged criticism. They focus on both pressing contemporary topics and historical issues that continue to define and inform the relationship between education and society.

As a term, *positions* refers to the obvious position that authors in the series take, but it might also refer to the "war of position" described by Italian cultural theorist Antonio Gramsci, who emphasized the centrality of political struggles over meanings, language, and ideas to the battle for civil society. We believe that these struggles over meanings, language, and ideas are crucial for the making of a more just social order in which political, cultural, and economic power is democratically controlled. We believe, as Paulo Freire emphasized, that there is no way not to take a position.

The current volume in the series, *Small Schools: Public School Reform Meets the Ownership Society*, takes the position

that the progressive grassroots educational reform movement
for small schools has been hijacked by business groups, right-
wing ideologues, and the ideology of the Ownership Society.
The small school ideal has long been viewed by its progressive
advocates not only as an effective educational reform but as
a means of reinvigorating community participation and the
civic role of public schooling and as being part of an attempt
to foster the formation of a broader democratic culture. Small
schools have been held up as offering not only a better model of
public school organization but as part of a radically democratic
alternative school model such as free schooling. As this book
disturbingly illustrates, ideologies of corporate culture, ever
more powerful right-wing think tanks, and the rise of neoliberal
philanthropy converge to transform the small schools vision
into the destructive long-standing agenda of privatization
advocates: draining public school resources to enrich investors,
attacking teachers' unions and teacher work, and assaulting
values of community and democratic participation. Part of
what is particularly valuable here is an examination of how
the political Right has done what appears to be a u-turn on
questions of centralized government authority when it comes
to public education. Conservative assaults on federalism in
public education long defended racial segregation and unequal
resource distribution in the name of local community. Yet,
the strong federal role under No Child Left Behind pushes
privatization and deregulation in the form of contracting,
charter schools, the testing industry, and sanctions. Federalism,
in this case, does not benefit local communities across the
nation but instead the tiny community of fiscal elites who own
the publishing, tutoring, and school-management companies.
This book intervenes in the ongoing and coordinated assault
on public goods and services from schools to housing and
shows how the undemocratic vision of the Ownership Society
must be countered with participatory democratic defense of

public institutions. The editors hope that this book—with information rich and fiercely argued—will be a clarion call for the reinvigoration of progressive and genuinely democratic forms of small schools: schools that can be places that make participatory democratic citizens not merely low wage workers and passive consumers paid principally by the unfulfillable fantasies of the Ownership Society.

KENNETH SALTMAN
ASSOCIATE PROFESSOR, EDUCATIONAL POLICY STUDIES AND RESEARCH
DEPAUL UNIVERSITY

RON SCAPP
PROFESSOR OF HUMANITIES AND TEACHER EDUCATION
THE COLLEGE OF MOUNT SAINT VINCENT

ACKNOWLEDGMENTS

We thank the many school reform activists, researchers, and educators who explore similar topics of inequities, power, and school reform. We should mention the work of Pedro Noguera, one of the regular speakers at our annual national Small Schools conference, who has challenged and inspired us. Then there's small-schools pioneer Deborah Meier, who has constantly cautioned us that, "small schools are not the answer, but without them none of the proposed answers stand a chance."

We made great use of the history of Chicago's corporate-led reform by Dorothy Shipps, *School Reform, Corporate Style: Chicago, 1880–2000* (Kansas); and of Elaine Garan's *In Defense of Our Children* (Heinemann), which offers a biting critique of current education policies in a popular Q&A style for parents and teachers. Then there's *Why Corporate America is Bashing Our Schools* (Heinemann), by fellow edblogger Susan Ohanian and Kathy Emery, and the prolific and provocative Gerald

Bracey who never gives an inch to the ownership society's "scientific research."

We offer our thanks to the many good friends and colleagues who have encouraged us, argued with us, fed us information, and explored these issues over dinners or libations. We can't begin to name you all. Gratitude to teachers Bill Armaline, Bill Ayers, Steve Barr, Sanders Bell, Timuel Black, Harold Brown, Leo Casey, Carl Davidson, Steve Jubb, Jon Kozol, Joe Kretovics, Trish McNeil, Joe Nathan, Bob Pearlman, Bill Schubert, Mike Stanton, Dan Swinney, and Madeline Talbott. Dana Vance provided early help with the research. Thanks to the Small Schools Workshop crew, and to the many members of the Small Schools Listserv, as well as to Small Talk blog readers who have contributed news, ideas, encouragement and provocative questions. To Aaron Dorfman of the National Committee for Responsive Philanthropy, thanks for sharing NCRP's uniquely valuable research and analytic expertise. Special thanks to our brother Fred Klonsky, teacher, thinker, union leader, and blogger extraordinaire.

Ken Saltman, scholar and editor of the Positions series, and Catherine Bernard, patient and persistent editor at Routledge, have encouraged us with their vision and solidarity

Thanks beyond measure to our three daughters: Jennifer, who teaches at Telpochcalli, a wonderful small school in Chicago's Little Village community; Amanda, who teaches poetry to youth in Chicago's juvenile detention center; Joanna, who writes about everything from kids and schools to world politics. (And thanks to Joanna for helping us with the damn endnotes.)

Finally, this book is lovingly dedicated to Oscar, our bravest, brightest, and most patient teacher.

INTRODUCTION
TWO TRAINS RUNNING

There is a time when the operation of the machine becomes so odious, makes you so sick at heart, that you can't take part; and you've got to put your bodies upon the gears and upon the wheels, upon the levers, upon all the apparatus and you've got to make it stop.

—Mario Savio, Sproul Plaza, December 3, 1964

It's always more challenging, risky, and more interesting, at least for this writer, to write about events as they are happening, rather than just looking in the rear view mirror; to write from the perspective of an active participant-observer rather than just observer. It's risky because there is always the chance—not chance, but certainty—that you are wrong about some things and will have to live down what you put on paper today. This book is intended not as a history of school reform and the Ownership Society, as this account takes place in the stretched present. We are all still living in the midst of both the Ownership Society culture and the continuing movement for reform: two trains running in opposite directions. Things change fast.

My own bent is toward journalism rather than history. However, I've been away from the field of journalism for many years, and the field has been greatly transformed, as have all fields, by the technological revolution. I posted two stories on my SmallTalk blog last May (three years ago, I knew nothing of blogs). The first came from a *New York Times* report detailing blatant discrimination against immigrant students in new public schools established under Mayor Bloomberg's small-schools reform. The second story was about a gathering of education management organizations (EMOs) and their supportive venture philanthropists in post-Katrina New Orleans. For us, the connection between the two stories transcended the fact that they occurred on the same day. A quote in Samuel Freedman's *Times* article by a leader of New York's immigrant's rights movement went so far as to tie the discriminatory policies directly to the No Child Left Behind (NCLB) Act. Ujju Aggarwal, an organizer for the Center for Immigrant Families, an advocacy group said:

> The situation...is not unique. Rather, it points to a proactive strategy fueled by No Child Left Behind, to continue to marginalize low-income children of color. By dismantling schools that have historically been under-resourced, into smaller schools under the pretense of "choice," immigrant children continue to be displaced by our public education system.

What a stinging condemnation of an idea, or rather an ideal, that many of us had held dear and for which we labored these last two decades. For us, small schools had seemed like the democratic alternative to the obsolete factory model of schooling with its chronic anonymity and filling-the-empty-vessel delivery system.

The small-schools movement held within it, it seemed to us, the possibilities for personalized, democratic, experiential, and relevant teaching. It offered the potential for schools that would be safer both physically and emotionally, with close, nurturing relationships between children and the adults who were teaching them. It also offered a possible alternative to segregation by race and class and the chance that students might be known by their assets, talents, dreams, and interests rather than by their deficits, family income, lack of prerequisites, or unstable family structures. In short, the movement held the promise that large, factory-style schools didn't and couldn't offer. Large high schools in particular were relics of a bygone age—the "smokestack society," as futurist Alvin Toffler tagged it. In the new information age, these schools seemed to us to be a caricature of the large factories that they mimicked and for which they trained future workers.

The obvious questions for long-time school reformers and small-schools educators and activists like us were: How could this have happened? How could the movement that we were a part of for so long and that we had helped to spawn have become transformed in such a way? How could our work, grounded in social-justice principles and democratic inquiry, gleaned from the Savio days, find common ground with education profiteers who excluded special-ed kids and English-language learners from their schools? And most important, could the movement still be saved and turned back around?

We began to explore the issue, at first from a local Chicago perspective in the February, 2006 issue of *The Phi Delta Kappan*, with a series of articles I coauthored with Small Schools Workshop founder Bill Ayers. The first essay was titled "Renaissance 2010: The Small Schools Movement Meets the Ownership Society."[1] Chicago Public Schools CEO Arne Duncan[2] and Coalition of Essential Schools Director Lewis Cohen[3] also contributed essays. Bill and I managed to get in the final word.[4] All four writers were avid small-schools advocates. However, our perspectives on the current situation were miles apart.

Our opening article raised the specter of an Ownership Society encroaching on Chicago's vaunted school reform, stealing its language and turning Mayor Daley's Renaissance 2010 plan to start 100 new small schools into a top-down strategy to close dozens of schools, primarily in the black community, and then turn them over to private management companies. Duncan denied that the new-schools plan had anything to do with union busting or privatization. "It's misleading to say that Renaissance 2010 is "turning over…new schools to private owners," wrote Duncan.

Technically, he was right. *Operators* would have been a better word than *owners*. Privately managed charters were still technically public schools. That's a point all too easily forgotten by many charter operators themselves. However, Duncan saw no difference between these schools he was bringing into town, which were run by charter management organizations (CMOs) such as Edison and Kipp, and those early small and charter schools started and run by teachers that had captured our imaginations a decade earlier. "School reform is not about creating winners and losers," he assured us, "but represents an effort to make every child in every school a winner." However, here he was, turning the school district into a new hierarchy of school types, charters, contract schools, performance schools, and just schools. Each category had its own level of autonomy and outside resources. Some had selective enrollments; some could spend twice the amount as the other, per student; some were given sparkling new facilities while others packed kids into 100-year-old buildings with stale air and bad food. No winners and losers, indeed. Even after school violence soared, largely as a result of the board's school-closing policies, which moved hundreds of kids across town to unprepared receiving schools, Duncan was unwilling to concede an inch to our argument.

Cohen of the Coalition of Essential Schools argued that school governance, private or public, wasn't an issue. What really counted in reform was "autonomy," he wrote. However, we asked, isn't autonomy largely an issue of governance, of power relationships? How could power relationships not be an issue? Autonomy for whom? Autonomy to do what? To us, small schools were largely about democracy in education. Could you really have democratic education and pedagogy in large, factory-model schools without democratic governance and a democratic culture? At what point does the autonomy granted to for-profit operators of public schools become a threat to that democratic vision and culture?

Was Duncan correct in ignoring our warning about the growing privatization threat or about the attack on public space taking place in our city? In the year that followed the publication of that special issue of *The Kappan*, the privatization trend in Chicago and most other large urban school districts has continued unabated. In the wake of Hurricane Katrina, which virtually erased its public school system, the city of New Orleans was turned into the new Mecca for for-profit charter management organizations. In New York, Mayor Bloomberg's reforms led to massive protests as new schools sprang up willy-nilly, many with selective enrollment policies, forcing large traditional schools to grow even larger while widening the already huge gap between the two classes of public schools. It soon came to light that many of the new public schools were actively and openly discriminating against kids with disabilities and those for whom English was a second language.

This book is partially a story about what happens when a promising, grass-roots movement for educational reform runs headlong into a powerful, conservative force that identifies itself as the Ownership Society. Each of these forces embodied different visions and dreams. Each claimed to be focused on freedom but, like two trains running in opposite directions, they were about two different kinds of freedom.

The first was about freedom from ignorance and inequality. It was a dream in which public education is a train leaving the station for the twenty-first century, where the neediest of kids would be equal passengers along with the most endowed. The dreamers were mostly educators and parents who were and still are prominent actors in the movement for urban school reform, a movement that has rocked large school systems from Miami to Los Angeles, from the battle against school segregation in the 1950s to the present. A small group of these dreamers helped to form the Small Schools Workshop in Chicago in 1991 in the midst of one of the most radical and far-reaching urban movements for social change since the Civil Rights Movement of the 1960s.

The second dream, couched in the same leave-no-child-behind rhetoric, was about the freedom of the marketplace and a consumer model of "choice," wherein perhaps instead of a train to the future, there stands a supermarket. The train still leaves the station for the new millennium, but the ridership is selective and segregated in different cars. Some advocates of choice equate school choice with choosing between an Apple iPod and another brand of MP3 player or between chunky and smooth peanut butter. Their dream is about a changing government role in our society in which the line between business and government gets blurred and ultimately disappears. The clearest manifestation of this dream is the military–industrial complex, a close and symbiotic relationship between the armed forces, private industry, and political interests and institutions, which President Eisenhower warned us about in his 1961 farewell address.

Ike, a Republican, worried about the growing influence of conservative extremists and about the danger of this massive complex making its "influence—economic, political, even spiritual—felt in every city, every statehouse, every office of the federal government." He was deeply concerned about the huge amounts of money flowing through government to self-interested and politically connected companies and the flow of managers back and forth, facilitating that flow. He feared that a handful of giant military industrialists would end up accumulating enormous power and be able to subvert the democratic processes, eliminating basic rights and freedoms and the reforms and social safety nets, like Social Security, that millions depended on for survival.

In a 1954 letter to his brother Edgar, he warned: "Should any political party attempt to abolish social security, unemployment insurance, and eliminate labor laws and farm programs, you would not hear of that party again in our political history."[5]

Many of us now worry that a similar complex is being forged, not at the Pentagon but down the road at the Department of Education. You could almost call it an educational–industrial complex, only with information-age contractors replacing the 1950's industrialists.

The small-schools movement, on its best days, held fast to the former dream. Its view of choice and autonomy had more to do with empowering teachers, students, parents, and communities than it did with putting peanut butter in the shopping cart. It was a fundamentally democratic movement that arose from the grass roots. In some ways, it was very traditional and community-based. In cities such as Chicago, the movement tried to shift decision-making authority out from under the big, centralized bureaucracy and down to the local school level. Its aim was in part to free local schools from unnecessary constraints, to allow for innovation and experimentation, and to engage whole communities, often for the first time, in decision making about their children's education.

All this made for strange but necessary bedfellows and for the creation of a broad coalition across ideological and partisan lines. Chicago's reform coalition included students, teachers, parents, community-based organizations and universities, and powerful business and philanthropic partners. Chicago's early school reform coalition came together around the ideas of educational equity, site-based management, school choice, and parental involvement. It led to the popular election of local school councils that were made up of parents, teachers, and community residents and had real powers. This first wave of reform took on several organizational forms and transcended traditional boundaries, embracing a range of political forces from the conservative Civic Committee of the Commercial Club of Chicago to the Chicago Teachers Union to various civil rights organizations.

School reform and coalition politics were nothing new to Chicago, the birthplace of community organizing. In fact, both go back almost as far as public education itself. However, as Dorothy Shipps[6] points out in her critical look at the city's corporate-style reform,

> Although Chicago made school reform history in the twentieth century, the performance of the system's large majority of black, Latino, and low-income students has not met reformers' expectations. This failure lies at the heart of a question facing urban school systems across the nation: why, despite a century of reform, have city schools failed to become what their citizens want?

Chicago's story, writes Shipps,

> challenges the conventional wisdom that state officials, school boards, and superintendents are initiators and sole implementers of urban reform and that greater bureaucratic accountability will increase the likelihood of success. Instead, it reveals school reform as part and parcel of urban coalition politics, initiated and sustained locally by business associations, unions, community-based organizations, good-government groups, and foundations.

Chicago's first-wave school reform coalition held together for nearly a decade, bringing many new improvements that would move the district from what former Secretary of Education William Bennett described in 1987 as the "worst in the nation" to what President Clinton upheld in his 1999 State of the Union address as a model for the whole nation to follow. Both perceptions, of course, were highly exaggerated.

However, the reform coalition couldn't hold together for long—not after Mayor Daley took over the Chicago school system in 1995. Less than a decade later, Daley, under pressure from Chicago's Civic Committee and with support of the world's largest foundation, succeeded in neutering the councils and much of the 1988 reform. By the 2000 election of George Bush, Chicago's reform would be a shadow of its former self, with the school district bowing to pressure from the conservative business sector to re-centralize, privatize, and dismantle the teachers' union.

By 2006, all but one or two of the dozen or so early school reform groups had been disbanded, their funding cut off by the local foundations. Chicago's philanthropists had bought into the mayor's Renaissance 2010 initiative to close "failing" neighborhood schools and to create 100 new schools, mainly charters and privately managed public schools, by the year 2010. That same year saw Arne Duncan make a pilgrimage to the U.S. Department of Education and swear allegiance to the NCLB, the same law and test-crazy policies that he had openly criticized a year earlier.

In August 2006, Civic Committee President R. Eden Martin published a commentary in the *Chicago Tribune* titled "End Chicago Public Schools Monopoly," signaling that the battle for the heart and soul of the city's school system was on. He attacked Chicago Public Schools as a "municipal monopoly" and claimed, without a shred of evidence, the superiority of teachers and students in charter schools. He especially liked the fact that charters weren't "constrained" by teacher collective-bargaining rights, as the Chicago Teachers Union (CTU) local was prohibited from representing teachers in Chicago's charter schools. The irony wasn't lost on us. Here was Martin, the embodiment of the Ownership Society in Chicago, the powerhouse lawyer from Sidley & Austin, who had made a career out of defending the country's largest monopolies in court, suddenly railing against the "municipal monopoly" of public education. Martin was a friend of big oil and an enemy of unions. He represented energy polluters and profiteering pharmaceutical companies. Where did he get the chutzpah to say anything about a "monopoly?" He loved monopolies. Why and how were he and his group calling the shots for Chicago's school reform?

When $100 million in Gates Foundation money came into the city, it changed the whole strategy of Chicago philanthropy, creating one big pot of cash that would be used to leverage "instructional change" from the top down. Like the all-encompassing federal NCLB Act, Chicago's reform would begin to de-emphasize individual school improvement in traditional schools and, instead, make a fetish of new-school and charter-school creation, closing "low-performing" schools, pulling the best students out of those schools and selectively enrolling them in charters and magnets, and bringing in outside agencies to run and replicate two-thirds of those new schools.

Two of the last surviving reform advocacy groups—Cross City Campaign for Urban School Reform, which kept a critical eye on the district's budget, and Neighborhood Capital Budget Group, which worked on capital spending and public school closings—closed their doors in 2007. With their departures, which were due mainly to the loss of foundation support, the fate of the first wave of reform was sealed. As Elizabeth Duffrin wrote in Chicago's reform journal *Catalyst*:

> The closings follow the demise in recent years of a number of school reform advocacy groups that supported local school councils, signaling a shift in Chicago's philanthropic and business leaders' views on how

best to invest their contributions to public education. More likely to pay
off, in their view, are direct investments in teacher training, curricula,
student learning and creating new schools... Less favored are advocacy
organizations that speak out on reform issues, but have limited impact.
Such groups are often "voices in the wilderness..."[7]

However, unlike these first-wave advocacy groups, the Small
Schools Workshop and the small-schools movement were
hardly the "voices in the wilderness" they had been a decade
earlier. The small-schools idea had gone from the margins to
the mainstream. By the mid-1990s, even Mayor Daley, who at
one time had pushed to close the city's first incarnations such
as Metro Alternative High School, had himself become a small-
schools advocate, recognizing in small, specialized schools of
choice the potential for attracting the middle class back into
the city from which it fled twenty-five years earlier. However,
it was becoming clear that his small-schools vision had little
resemblance to ours.

Though federal funding for public schools made up a
relatively small piece of the pie, there was never a time when
White House politics and priorities had been as invasive as
those of the Bush administration. Though the NCLB law was a
product of bipartisan machinations, it became the centerpiece
of a destructive conservative agenda that in this book we call
the Ownership Society. We didn't make up the name. It was a
George W. Bush campaign slogan. However, we found it a useful
way to talk about the important social, political, and economic
changes that were taking place all around us. Besides, if Bush
could use and redefine our movement's no-child language, why
couldn't we use his? Throughout this book, we set Ownership
Society in caps to identify the specific major policy and cultural
shift brought on in the wake of the 2000 elections and the
accession to power of the neo-cons.

Among the key elements of the Ownership Society in the arena of education policy have been a single-minded reliance on high-stakes standardized test scores, plus a punitive approach to low-performing schools, combined with chaotic student transfer provisions, all of which have served to undermine reform efforts in city after city. Even in Chicago, an unwavering Democratic city (except for that brief period in 1983 when Harold Washington became the Democratic Party's candidate for mayor and the majority of white Daley Democrats turned Republican overnight), the city's education leaders were quick in rendering unto Caesar—and accepting the terms of the NCLB.

Soon the language of accountability and easily measurable standardization replaced that of equity and building smaller learning communities. In cities such as New York and Chicago, the old reform coalitions built on community engagement began to take on the manner of a top-down business model under Mayor Bloomberg and Chancellor Klein, and the heart of reform was punctured.

The war in Iraq has drained education budgets and threatened civil and human rights and broad areas of public space, both here and abroad. Published results from the ongoing hearings into the Department of Education's Reading First and student-loan scandals should be more than enough to fill several books with exposures of the discredited policies and politics of the Ownership Society crowd now running the Department of Education.

However, it strikes us as quite remarkable that there are still so many people, including educational reformers, who easily see through the current administration's propaganda coming from the Pentagon but continue to trust their good intentions when it comes from across the river at Department of Education. Understandably, those who have benefited the most from the Ownership Society's educational privatization strategies trust most readily.

We aren't anti-corporatists opposed to all entrepreneurial ventures, all private investment, or private partnerships in education. In fact, we think there should be more of those partnerships and even greater reinvestment in cities such as Chicago and a consideration of new forms of both social and private ownership. The corporations put great demands on public education and exercise, either directly or through their foundations, civic organizations, and think tanks, great influence over education policies and politics without contributing their fair share of the tax burden.

If and when a new administration replaces the current Ownership Society faction in Congress and in the White House, and as a new reform coalition is built, business will of course, have a seat at the table—but hopefully not the only seat, or even the biggest seat. When we, a group of educators and high school reform activists, asked for such a seat when the Gates Foundation first created its shadow board to oversee its initial $50 million investment in Chicago's new small schools, we were told by one of the foundation leaders: "No. That would be a conflict of interests. Like having the workers running the factory." Such is the contested nature of urban school reform.

As we continue to point out, school reform was, and continues to be, contested territory. In cities such as Chicago, the democratic elements within the reform movement appear to have taken a back seat while the interests of the Ownership Society are driving the bus. However, if public education is to successfully address long-standing issues of equity and quality for all children, there needs to be common ground around an agenda and a vision that can bring together traditional civic leaders and grassroots groups, teachers, parents, and students in a new coalition capable of transcending the narrow limitations imposed by narrow conservative frameworks and alliances.

Susan and I are both educators, parents of public school students, and active participants in a historic movement to transform the content and conduct of public education. We are writing in large measure about personal and collective experiences that now stretch from civil rights and educational activism in the mid-1960s to the present. For us, that present is mainly an extension of that world-changing movement that we were a part of forty years ago as student activists and in which we continue to work today. We have used what there is of current research to deepen our critique of the Ownership Society and of current school reform trends.

In the following chapters, we review the history of the early small-schools and charter movement and show how they were undermined by powerful conservative influences. We go on to define the Ownership Society, its culture and its driving forces, and describe its impact on all areas of society, especially its assault on public space and democratic values. We can't help but devote chapters to the roles played by conservative think tanks and the rise of the new power philanthropists, the brains and money behind the Ownership Society. Finally, we offer up what we hope are some useful suggestions for strategies for building new school reform coalitions and alternatives to current top-down reform initiatives.

We have seasoned our argument with stories from the media, from interviews with educators and reform activists, and from our own experiences. We hope this book can contribute something to the work and struggle of educators and others who believe in the worthiness of the cause of democratic education in a democratic society. It's never easy to write a book collectively and collaboratively. We have somehow managed to write and work together on various projects over the last forty years without doing irreparable harm to our marriage. However, as we tell our friends, "We are professionals; don't try this at home."

MIKE KLONSKY

1

THE SMALL-SCHOOLS MOVEMENT
MEETS THE OWNERSHIP SOCIETY

The future ain't what it used to be.
—Yogi Berra

The small-schools movement was probably misnamed. It was never really just about "small." Some social theorists, such as economist E.F. Schumacher, saw great value in small things. However, what captured the vision of many urban educators as they moved into the new millennium were the traditional democratic values of Deweyan progressivism combined with Information Age notions of professional community, personalization, and safe learning environments in an unsafe society.

Many of these small-school ideas emerged from the theories and practices of the civil-rights movement of the 1960s, its Freedom Schools and Citizenship Schools and the not-unrelated explosion of alternative schools during that same decade. Among the big ideas of that period were the notions that access to a purposeful, high-quality public education for all children was a democratic right worth fighting for and that the definition of *public* was contested territory; that teaching-learning was and always had been organically tied to social change and social justice. It was no accident that many of the new wave of school reform and urban small-school leaders during the next three decades would come from the ranks of the civil-rights movement. Nor was it surprising that a large contingent of these new small schools would explicitly define themselves as "schools of social justice." Like many of the themed small schools, social justice high schools offered a way of connecting the core curriculum with the passions and interests of students, especially those from inner-city schools who, almost daily, had to confront issues of inequity, war, and violence, and who sought ways of reshaping the world in which they would grow to maturity. The movement's impact was felt from the plantation South to urban communities in New York, Philadelphia, and Chicago.

The idea was not just to make schools smaller but to capture two essentials for successful learning: (1) the visibility of children and (2) the professional community of teachers. The first meant that school environments and practices would facilitate closer, stronger relationships between kids and adults; that every student would be known by a group of caring, nurturing adults; that students would be active participants and not just receptacles in the creation of knowledge; and that anonymity was enemy number one.

The second meant that smaller schools would enable collaboration among teachers, collaboration across the traditional grade and departmental lines. Faculty meetings of 150–300 teachers, with the principal and a few administrators or faculty leaders doing all the talking, would be no more. Instead, a team of teachers, small enough to fit around a good-sized table, would have the time to meet together regularly, to plan integrated lessons, to look at student work together, to observe and critically assess each other's teaching, and to initiate and mentor young teachers into the profession.

These new small schools could take on many and varied forms. Some were designed from scratch as freestanding, completely autonomous schools. Others were schools-within-a-school or several schools, sharing one facility. Some advocates compared it to an office building, home to several distinct and unique businesses and sharing a common eating facility and maintenance and building security and perhaps shared cable or wireless services. Use of the common auditorium could be scheduled through a coordinator, but the autonomy of each business would be held sacrosanct.

We took from futurist Alvin Toffler the image of immutable, huge, and bureaucratic economic, social, and political systems of the industrial age being dragged kicking and screaming into the knowledge-based world of the twenty-first century. From Ted Sizer, former dean of the Harvard Graduate School of Education and the founder of the Coalition of Essential Schools, we learned to think that less might be more when it came to thinking about curriculum or that the trade-off of curricular breadth for depth would be worth considering. Says Sizer:

> We didn't come up with a model. We came up with a set of very simple ideas which reflected the compromises that [high school teacher] Horace had to make. We said no high school should ask a teacher to be responsible for more than 80 youngsters at once. We said kids should be promoted not because they get older, but because they exhibit real mastery of their work. So, what counted was what the kids could show us they could do, rather then just that they had collected credits in

courses that they might or might not have learned anything in. These were simple, common-sense ideas, but very counter cultural.[1]

Such subversive ideas were incorporated into a list of ten principals that influenced the way many of us began thinking about possibilities in new smaller schools.[2]

Another big-idea dreamer was Toffler's counterpart in the world of information technology, Bill Gates. It's hard for us to say for sure whether the world's richest man has been part of the problem or part of the solution. When it comes down to such individuals, its difficult to even know the Metric. Often, visionary reformers are elitists who become exasperated with the slow pace of change and with the difficult but necessary community organizing and engagement work needed for deep-going social transformation. They rely only on the power of their own ideas or on the latest business fad, backed up with billionaire wealth—their own or other people's—to drive top-down versions of change.

Time magazine purported to tell us how to bring our schools out of the twentieth century. They began with, "a dark little joke exchanged by educators with a dissident streak:"[3]

Rip Van Winkle awakens in the 21st century after a hundred-year snooze and is, of course, utterly bewildered by what he sees. Men and women dash about, talking to small metal devices pinned to their ears. Young people sit at home on sofas, moving miniature athletes around on electronic screens. Older folk defy death and disability with metronomes in their chests and with hips made of metal and plastic. Airports, hospitals, and shopping malls—every place Rip goes just baffles him. But when he finally walks into a schoolroom, the old man knows exactly where he is. "This is a school," he declares. "We used to have these back in 1906. Only now the blackboards are green."

For the *Time* writers, the Rip Van Winkle story is a parable:

This is a story about the big public conversation the nation is not having about education, the one that will ultimately determine not merely whether some fraction of our children get "left behind" but also whether an entire generation of kids will fail to make the grade in the global economy because they can't think their way through abstract problems, work in teams, distinguish good information from bad or speak a language other than English.

The lore of public school failure is so powerful and overwhelming that it makes many well-meaning people ask whether saving and reforming public schools is even possible. And, if it is, is it worth the trouble? For *Time*, it becomes relatively easy to slide in the lingo of the Ownership Society, of the "global economy," of the real possibility of some kids—or even an entire generation—failing to "make the grade" (see how easily grades fit in with sorting and deciding who gets "left behind").

Though we doubt that kids back in 1906 ever heard of a global economy, the role of public school bureaucracies as mechanisms for sorting and tracking is now accepted as undeniable fact and, hopefully, the need for change even more so. There's not much sense in trying to defend public schools as a group any more than trying to attack them as a group. Public schools have long been the backbone of a democratic society and will continue to be so. Though we don't buy into the notion of public school "failure," we do see a poorly supported system that can't hope to meet the educational needs of its neediest citizens under present conditions.

The *Time* writer failed to grasp how much things have changed in schools since the turn of the century. Public schools back then were mainly small and rural. There's no way Rip would recognize today's mega high schools in cities such as Miami, Los Angeles, or New York, with their student populations of 3,000 or more per school (such vast size was also the work of such reformers as James Conant, by the way).

Today's wireless computing, students with iphones, graphing calculators, ability groups, high-stakes standardized testing, punishing schools for low test scores, teachers unions, and talk of "competing in the global economy" plus the absence of hickory sticks and floggings—all would make Rip scratch his pillow-napped head.

However, the real mind-blower for him might be to see classrooms filled with African-American and Latino kids having the legal right to attend public schools, along with a mix of immigrants speaking dozens of languages and children with all sorts of disabilities nationwide. After all, public schools at the turn of the twentieth century didn't have a mission to educate all children.

Rip's feelings of déjà vu would probably be stronger in those urban and rural schools populated by the nation's poorest kids, schools where the blackboards haven't changed color—only the children's faces have. In wealthy suburban districts such as Winnetka (IL) or Scarsdale (NY), Rip would be completely lost in modern classrooms where even blackboards are an anomaly amid the maze of instructional technology, science labs, white boards, atria and food courts, carpeted locker rooms adjoining modern workout gyms, kids with their own laptops and PDAs.

Tales of public school failure and immutability are both true and false. It's true that public schools are difficult to change, especially from the top down. The pace of incremental school change can be glacial. However, that's also true of modern bureaucratic systems in general, from the Kremlin to the Pentagon and from our health care system to environmental protection. The lore of the permanence and immutability of large public systems can be used either way: as a catalyst for revolutionary change or, more typically, as a driver of top-down, undemocratic (inevitably unsuccessful) change initiatives.

Privatization strategies aim at eroding or selling off public space and, with it, public decision making. When public schools are run by outside companies, it's those companies—not teachers or parents—that make the most important decisions about the purpose, process, and product of schooling. Almost by default, new information-age entrepreneurs reproduce the old factory-model relationships between teachers and their managers. A class of outside contractors has now captured new small-by-design schools, originally envisioned as professional communities. The aim of education, the purpose of schooling, now becomes the profitability of the management company or, in the bigger world, America's success in the global economy.

Public bureaucracies are replaced by new private ones. Or there's always the easy solution—changing the name, the sign above the schoolhouse door or the very language of schooling, as when the superintendent of Pittsburgh's public schools took the word *public* off the district letterhead in an effort to "raise the image" of the school system in a ludicrous attempt to distance the school system from its own reputation and lure back the very class of people who first abandoned the system rather than send their kids to school with the other.

In 2002, after taking control of the city's public schools, New York's Mayor Bloomberg famously demolished the thirty-two public school subdistricts that came out of the city's 1968 school governance reorganization, replacing them with ten regional superintendents who reported to the deputy chancellor, who reported to the chancellor, who reported to the mayor. Bloomberg proceeded to abolish that whole structure in 2007, replacing it with a bevy of private and nonprofit management companies to oversee local schools.

"This system was intentionally top-down," said Chancellor Joel Klein. "The goal was taming the system and bringing all of the teachers, principals, and administrators onto the same page."[4] Taming indeed. Same page, indeed. As these new Siegfrieds and Roys would find out, public education is and always was a battlefield, contested territory, with no "taming" allowed.

Chicago's 1988 School Reform Act decentralized decision making, shifting major areas of authority from the central administration down to the local school level. The law passed, thanks to the strong backing of the business community, represented by such organizations as the Civic Committee and the Chamber of Commerce. Their support for the new law was a response to the election of the city's first black mayor, Harold Washington, and a period in which much of the city's black middle class found positions in teaching or administrative positions with the public school system. Suddenly, the white business community became disenchanted with bloated bureaucracies. Now we needed a law to break the hold of the central office over the local schools. That was accomplished with the 1988 reform act and the accession to power, once again, of the Daley political machine. Predictably, these same groups now clamor for more centralization and a swing back to top-down decision making by the mayor.

School failure lore also masks what Jonathan Kozol has so well characterized as "Savage Inequalities," the vastly unequal distribution of resources that create the two tiers of public schooling: one tier, a pathway to the global economy, and the other, a pathway to menial jobs, unemployment, or jail. The *Time* story preceded by a week another Blue Ribbon report. This one, right from the heart of the Ownership Society, was published by something called the "New Commission on the Skills of the American Workforce"[5] and was hailed as the greatest document since the 1983 Nation at Risk Report. (I'm sure, by the time this book is published, this report will be long forgotten and a new one will be being prepared, warning us about some new crisis or invasion by illegal immigrants or by a new foreign power.)

The New Commission included executives from Viacom, Inc. and Lucent Technologies and school officials from New York,

Massachusetts, and California along with Mayor Bloomberg and former Michigan governor John Engler, now president of the National Association of Manufacturers. The Annie E. Casey Foundation, the Bill and Melinda Gates Foundation, the William and Flora Hewlett Foundation, and the Lumina Foundation funded it. The report followed others with such names as "Rising Above the Gathering Storm" and "America's Perfect Storm: Three Forces Changing Our Nation's Future." Though each report differed in authorship and focus, all shared the same dire picture of public education connected with the same alarmist view about America's economic future.

The report damned the public schools as "obsolete" for failing to prepare young people to compete in the global market place and blamed the public education system for the market gains made by other competing nations. Proposed solutions ranged from pie-in-the-sky ("enable every member of the adult workforce to get the new literacy skills") to the farcical ("create regional competitiveness authorities to make America competitive") to the profitable ("change state law to allow districts to turn over the day-to-day operations of their schools to private contractors"). Nothing much was made of the decrepit living conditions in blighted communities, urban and rural, or about the vast inequities that mark the system's distribution of resources or qualified teachers. Nor is there an explanation of how taking more math classes is going to help graduates find jobs as, say, tool-and-die makers, when so much of tool-and-die work computation is being done with computers, not to mention the fact that nearly all such jobs are being exported to countries where skilled workers can be hired at lower wages.

The idea of small learning communities might have had a familiar ring to old Rip, as it borrowed some from the old one-room schoolhouses and town hall meetings of his day. However, the modern small schools movement is no mere nostalgic throwback. In urban districts, it can probably be traced back to the mid-1970s and the emergence of several small-by-design schools in New York, most notably, Deborah Meier's Central Park East Elementary and Secondary Schools, founded in 1974 in East Harlem's District 4. Sy Fliegel, the director of the district's alternative schools, christened Central Park East the "Miracle in East Harlem" in his book of the same name.[6] However, Central Park East was no miracle. It was the product of a strong vision and lots of hard work on the part of a team of committed educators. Good small schools were the work of human beings here on earth, not divine providence.

What started as a noble experiment in democratic education by New York teachers would grow over the next thirty years into the most dramatic reform of public education since school desegregation and the 1954 case of Brown v. Board of Education. Meier and other original New York small-schoolers took their inspiration from contemporary social-justice and democratic movements, as we also did in Chicago. The struggle against southern school segregation produced what came to be known as the Freedom Schools or Citizenship Schools. Educators such as Septima Poinsette Clark, Bernice Robinson, Highlander Folk School, and the Southern Christian Leadership Conference established the first small Citizenship Schools, teaching reading to adults across the Deep South. The schools were created in part to circumvent legal barriers that were set up by segregationists— literacy tests and quizzes on interpreting the Constitution—that were set up for the sole purpose of preventing black citizens from voting.[7]

In the summer of 1964, more than forty freedom schools were opened in Mississippi by a host of groups such as the Student Nonviolent Coordinating Committee (SNCC), Council of Federated Organizations (COFO), the Southern Christian Leadership Conference, and the National Association for the Advancement of Colored People. The schools were a part of

Freedom Summer, which brought hundreds of civil rights workers to the state from campuses nationwide. Educators and activists such as Dorothy Cotton, Robert Moses, Staughton Lynd, Stokely Carmichael, Charles Cobb, and Ella Baker created these schools inside churches, on people's back porches, or out in the fields and farms of Mississippi, Alabama, and Georgia. The schools became centers of organizing and an integral part of the whole freedom movement.[8]

In the North about the same time, a movement of progressive educators was experimenting with alternatives to traditional and factory-school schools. Many of these experiments took place outside the public school system and targeted kids who had fallen through the cracks or into the gaping holes in the traditional system. Models ranged from Montessori, School Without Walls, Waldorf, and Summerhill to the more practical Comer Process schools, which soon found their way inside the public school system.

In the midst of Chicago's path-breaking school reform, which decentralized the third largest public school system in the United States, groups of autonomy-seeking teachers approached the Small Schools Workshop and other organizations, seeking assistance in developing a group of small public schools. A large coalition gradually took shape and, working in partnership with the Chicago Public Schools system and the Chicago Teachers Union Quest Center, ultimately helped to launch more than 130 small urban schools or learning communities across the city.

Bill Ayers, a radical reform activist and professor at the University of Illinois at Chicago's College of Education, founded the Small Schools Workshop in 1991. The Workshop's mission was to support teachers' restructuring efforts in large, overcrowded schools. Its work also consisted of developing a research base to support that work. Findings included a strong correlation between school size and low student achievement; high dropout rates; increased school violence; use of drugs, alcohol, and tobacco on the part of adolescents; and other anti-societal and self-destructive behaviors (Ford & Klonsky, 1994; Klonsky, 1995).[9-12] Working closely with researchers, policy makers, and groups of public school teachers, the Workshop helped to create an incubator for new small schools and heightened new public awareness of the benefits of these smaller learning communities.

One of the great benefits arising from Chicago's far-reaching school reform was that decentralization opened up schools to observation, research, and evaluation. The air was filled with lively debate and community discussions as researchers from around the country traveled to Chicago to jointly study the "revolution" that was taking place. Researchers such as Michael Katz, Michelle Fine, and Elaine Simon[10] were among the first outside researchers who wondered how such a radical reform as elected local school councils made up of parents, teachers, and community members could have received so little national media attention when they knew how resistant school bureaucracies could be to reform. As it turns out, the three may have overestimated the staying power of Chicago reform, which has been all but reversed since Mayor Daley's takeover of the school system in 1995. However, at the time, the new transparency proved to be a threat not only to bureaucratic management, but to those who were improperly profiting from it. Even the president of the board of education was ultimately indicted, tried, and sent to prison.

Researchers from the University of Chicago's Consortium on Chicago School Research and the Bank Street College of Education revealed that school size was playing a significant role in determining which schools were actually improving; producing better learning outcomes and safer, more friendly environments; and offering students more authentic and intellectually challenging experiences. Their 1999 report concluded: "In Chicago…there is a democratic movement across sectors in which adults and children, inside and beyond public schools, recognize that public education is indeed a collective, urban responsibility."[11] How times have changed. In today's environment, these words do sound almost revolutionary.

That early research also revealed a decrease in levels of school violence and disruptive behavior and higher levels of parent involvement and teacher collaboration when school size was reduced and students were part of a small learning community. The Bank Street report concluded that though small size may not have been a "panacea," it was "an important facilitative factor when adults are predisposed to advance improvement efforts. From a system perspective, encouraging the development of small schools is one important element in a larger array of strategies that would help create conditions that foster improvement."

We started the Small Schools Workshop with just such a perspective. We didn't see smaller schools as a cure-all but as a strategy for encouraging systemic change and community engagement. Our goal was to support teachers and community groups as they worked to create new, smaller learning communities in a historically toxic educational environment for poor kids and children of color—in a school system generally immune to substantial change initiatives, a system with a legacy of racial discrimination, segregation, corruption, and neglect.

Though the small-schools movement at that time represented a wide range of political and educational philosophies, its vision was closely connected to issues of social justice, equity, and community. Small schools were not seen as some new efficiency or technical ramp-up. They represented not a "taming" or reining-in of teachers and principals but an unleashing, a means to liberate talents and energies. Neither were small schools intended as some new, sophisticated mechanism for sorting and tracking students. Rather, they offered a strategy for engaging teachers, students, parents, and whole communities (i.e., the people with the problems).

Since then, the movement has grown nationally and has many victories under its belt. In Chicago, dozens of small schools have been created from the ground up, and several large high schools have been started on the road to restructuring. Elected local school councils were shown to be responsible in widespread improvement across 144 elementary schools, especially compared with schools that had been targets of top-down interventions by the district's central office.[12]

The results of Chicago's decentralization and of its early small-school movement have been mainly positive, producing stronger relationships between teachers and students, lower dropout and mobility rates, safer school environments and, to a lesser degree, improved test scores. However, like most comprehensive reform initiatives, the gains were largely dependent on and limited by the ability of schools to implement stability of leadership, adequate time and resources for teachers' planning, and professional development. Several attempts to restructure large high schools were abandoned in mid-course or reversed, with the inevitable shifts in administrative policy or leadership. At Chicago Vocational High School (CVS), one of the largest and most troubled high schools in the district, Principal Betty Despenza-Green led the first small-schools restructuring initiative. Within five years, following the creation of seven small academies, CVS was named one of the top five New Urban High Schools by the Department of Education. However, after Dr. Green's retirement four years later, a new principal was appointed and quickly disbanded the small schools. CVS was soon back to where it was, plagued by school violence and high dropout rates. We were left with the image of an unfinished skyway, jutting out across the bay.

The small-schools movement in Chicago began in the early 1990s and twenty years earlier in New York. However, the first major shift in national policy toward smaller public schools came in the wake of the horrific shootings at Columbine High School in Colorado in 1999. That event refocused school reform efforts nationally, for the first time, on the high schools. Columbine was a large high school of nearly 2,000 kids. Its predominantly white population and affluent suburban setting made the shootings front-page news around the world.

A side note: As we are writing this book, the Chicago papers carry the story of Roberto Duran, a fourteen-year-old student at one of the city's excellent small high schools. Roberto became the twenty-fourth Chicago Public Schools student killed by gun violence during the 2006–07 school year. He wasn't shot inside the school, and there was the usual speculation, as with the twenty-three who were shot before him, that he was a victim of "gang violence." That's usually all it takes to relegate the dead student and the young shooter to the back pages of anonymity. Columbine was shut down for months after the shootings. Camera crews, clergy, and government teams poured into Littleton, Colorado to minister to the survivors and to report every sad detail of the murder-suicide and its aftermath. The school's modern, well-equipped library, scene of much of the rampage, was torn down and completely rebuilt so that students would be spared the pain associated with revisiting the scene of the crime. An 11,000-page report on the event was released nineteen months after the shooting.

The hundreds of inner-city youths killed in violent episodes in and outside of schools are never remembered that long after the killings take place, except by those who loved them. Rarely is there a bio or a face attached to the name of either the victim or of the perpetrator. For the victim, school may have even been a relatively safe haven from tough inner-city streets. However, that's a story that goes untold.

Every day in America, 14,000 young people are victims of violence. Teenagers are twice as likely as any other people to be shot, stabbed, sexually assaulted, beaten, or otherwise attacked. When we think about crime, we tend to think about teenagers as perpetrators. However, far more teens are victimized by crime than are victimizers. Though many teenagers live in homes where domestic violence exists, they also may attend schools where bullying is prevalent, or they may inhabit neighborhoods where street gangs are the main form of social organization and where violence is a fact of daily life.

A survey of urban school climate by the National School Boards Association's Council of Urban Boards of Education found that a majority of students say they feel safe in their school, an indicator that experts say improves academic achievement. According to the 2006 survey, almost 63 percent of urban students report feeling safe at school. However, nearly 20 percent of students believe that other students carry weapons in school. Students in grades 9–12 expressed even more concern over weapons, with more than 40 percent not sure whether others came to school armed. This is an improvement over the period around the Columbine shootings, when surveys conducted by the Horatio Alger Association of Distinguished Americans found that the number of public school students who said they always feel safe in school fell from 44 percent in 1998 to 37 percent in 1999 and, in a Wall Street Journal–NBC News survey on social issues, 58 percent ranked youth violence as their top concern. This, even though there was a reported decline in school violence during those same years. Why do students feel greater anxiety even though the numbers tell them they are safer? Maybe the numbers don't tell the whole story.

Following the Columbine shootings, Congress, in a rare bipartisan move, appropriated $48 million for creating smaller learning communities (SLCs) in large high schools. The basic idea behind the Smaller Learning Communities authorizing legislation was that the personalization and stronger relationships common to smaller learning communities would make schools safer—and they did. The 2001 SLC allotment was set at $125 million. This federal initiative also drove millions of dollars in private funding initiatives, ultimately including nearly $1.5 billion in grants from the Bill and Melinda Gates Foundation, earmarked for the creation of new small public schools.

The U.S. Department of Education Office of Vocational and Adult Education, led by Assistant Secretary of Education Patricia McNeil, serving under then-Secretary Richard Riley, managed the SLC grants, begun under the Clinton administration. Riley was an avid supporter of the small-schools idea, as were the Clintons. McNeil, through her work in education-to-career programs, saw the potential of learning communities within otherwise large high schools to engage students in meaningful schoolwork and help them on their way to higher education or the world of work (or both). After her stint in Washington, McNeil moved to Colorado and became a coach and advocate for SLCs, working with schools districts around the country to support high school redesign projects.

However, the changes in the Department of Education under Bush appointee Rod Paige marked a big shift from the Clinton-Riley era, challenging the very existence of high school transformation and the SLC grant program. SLC funds, along with various major funds for vocational education, were stripped from each annual K–12 budget. With the passage of the No Child Left Behind (NCLB) act came a dramatic reordering of priorities. Hillary Clinton, who like most Democrats had voted for NCLB and now regretful over what she called the "broken promises" of the Bush administration that had defunded high school reform, lashed out at the cuts:

> One of the goals of the No Child Left Behind act is to ensure that all students receive the education and services needed in order to compete in the 21st century market place. Despite this fact, the

President has proposed to eliminate programs targeted at improving the performance of students that are most at risk of not receiving a college education. These programs include the Vocational and technical education ($1.3 billion), GEAR UP ($303 million), three TRIO programs—Talent Search ($145 million), Upward Bound ($278 million) and Upward Bound Math/Science ($33 million), and Smaller Learning Communities ($94 million).[13]

Under Secretary Paige's leadership, federal funds were shifted in the direction of increased support for private schools and privately managed charters. Even though the funding was partially restored in various compromise versions of the budget, the shift in Department of Education focus was significant. It reflected a yawning difference between those who believed public schools needed to be and could be reformed and those who believed reform was either impossible or too difficult. It showed those of us in the small-schools movement that we were skating on thin ice and that our ability to help to create the hundreds of new small schools we had envisioned, with government support, was in jeopardy.

The NCLB act focused on offering some student and parents escape routes from traditional public schools rather than providing resources, strategies, or support for improving those schools they left behind. Under NCLB, elementary schools that failed for two consecutive years to make "adequate yearly progress" could lose their highest-scoring kids and their remaining middle-class base as a de facto punishment for having too many poor kids. High schools were not even included in the law.

In the early days of the small-schools movement, restructuring was thought of as something positive, as the highest form of school reform because it was comprehensive, rather than piecemeal, tinkering. Schools that were doing restructuring were on the cutting edge of reform. Flash forward to the present period of privatization, NCLB, and the Ownership Society and restructuring has become a four-letter word. AP writer Nancy Zuckerbrod, makes the point well in a recent *Time* story:

> The scarlet letter in education these days is an "R." It stands for restructuring—the purgatory that schools are pushed into if they fail to meet testing goals for six straight years under the No Child Left Behind law...The schools bearing the label are often in poor urban areas, like Far Rockaway at the end of the subway line in the New York City borough of Queens... Only schools that receive federal aid for low-income students—known as Title I—are subject to the law's consequences.[14]

Here was a policy that, despite its grandiose title and mission statement, couldn't help but leave the great majority of poorer kids and families behind. In reality, NCLB was part of a strategy to drive the demographic shifts necessary for the transformation of the economy and transformation of communities, to facilitate the badly needed migration of a technically skilled workforce back into urban centers of finance and information technology. This shift was also largely responsible for the real estate boom of the last decade, a boom that may be about to play itself out in condo-glutted changing urban neighborhoods and neatly groomed suburban communities.

Students with special needs and disabilities, immigrants, and English-language learners became all but expendable in the test score race. While the federal NCLB law didn't specify what kind of instruction schools should use for English-language learners, many schools across the country, swept up in a wave of anti-immigrant political fervor, discontinued or limited their bilingual education.

The NCLB put pressure on schools to show strong test scores in lower grades, even though it often takes several years for students in bilingual programs to perform at or above grade level in either or both languages. Many of the new small schools in New York and Chicago consciously avoided recruitment of ELL (English language learner) students, particularly during the start-up years of new schools.

In several urban districts, a congressionally mandated experiment with charter schools began to take root, surrounding poor, under-resourced neighborhood schools and attracting higher-scoring kids and the dollars that followed them. In Washington, D.C., a decade of top-down reform meant that one-fourth of public school students were attending the city's fifty-five charters, and because funding follows the students, regular public schools with shrinking enrollment were being stripped of funds.

MacFarland Middle School, for example, saw its enrollment drop from more than 600 to about 300 in two years. MacFarland's principal gave her perspective to *Washington Post* writers: "'I don't try to compete with them anymore,' said Antonia Peters, in her ninth year as MacFarland's principal. 'I try to work with the kids that we have. Most of my students are ELL or special education, but they take the same test as mainstream kids in English. It's hard if you don't know the language or have special needs, but we're held to the same standards.'"[15]

In Chicago, shifts in school policies running counter to the first wave of reform came from two sources: (1) the growing penetration of the NCLB and the Department of Education's punitive testing pressures and the 1995 shift to mayoral control of the school system, which reversed decentralization, and (2) concentrated power put back in the hands of the Civic Committee. The Civic Committee is the policy arm of the elite Commercial Club, the gathering place of the most powerful corporate forces in the city for the last 125 years. The Civic Committee has often played the role of local conservative, business-oriented think tank, only without the usual buffer zone between direct corporate interests and politicians that you find with the think tanks in Chapter 5.

The Commercial Club has historically played an active role in shaping and reforming the city's public education system and often exercised control over the school system's budget and financing. It has also been the business community's bulwark against Chicago's militant union movement. The Club was always a manifestation of the battlefield of competing interests over control of public schools, according to historian Dorothy Shipps:

> Club members self-righteously believed that the rapidly growing public schools could simultaneously upgrade the masses, preserve order, and provide young workers. They sought to vocationalize, economize, and rationalize schooling, steering it by judicious application of the same governing principles they thought best for their own businesses: keep taxes low, organize the work "scientifically," and, above all trust in management. Labor groups provided an alternative vision of schooling that emphasized worker democracy in governance, social change through education, and equal access for all students to the highest levels of public schooling.[16]

Emboldened by the Ownership Society culture emanating from Washington, the Civic Committee soon grew weary of the very school decentralization they had earlier supported. The Committee became more aggressive in pushing for privatization and union-busting initiatives, which would lead to the closing of dozens of neighborhood schools and their replacement with privately managed charter schools.

They offered the mayor a new plan for reform, their version of the mayor's own Renaissance 2010 plan, in a June 2003 report called *Left Behind*.[17] The report called for the creation of 100 new schools over the next decade, most of which would be charter schools, devoid of unions and collective bargaining rights for teachers. The report briefly mentioned the high poverty rates among the 430,000 Chicago Public School children but brushed aside any notion that there could be a connection between poverty and measurable learning outcomes, saying only that, "poverty and ethnicity are not educational straitjackets."

This curt, matter-of-fact statement flew in the face of nearly all previous research, which showed beyond a reasonable doubt that poverty, particularly in isolated minority communities, was indeed an educational "straitjacket" and correlated with the lack of social capital in the lives of the poor and minority students and in their concentration in resource-poor schools. A poor African-American student in Chicago, for example, was twice as likely as a white student to have an inexperienced teacher in his or her classroom. The Civic Committee report also cleared top school executives, the mayor, and the Board of Education of any and all responsibility for the declining state of affairs they were reporting at Chicago Public Schools (CPS):

> As citizens ponder these implications, it is essential to keep in mind that this failure is not attributable to the current CEO of the system or to its board. There is probably no more dedicated or talented CEO of a major urban school system in the country than Chicago's current CEO. The same could be said of the members of the Board—all intelligent, conscientious volunteers in public service.[18]

So, if neither poverty nor the poor leadership of the school district was to blame, who or what should bear the onus of the supposed failure of Chicago's public schools? Obviously, it was the teachers, the parents, and the children themselves. The Committee offered that it "was a lack of competition" within the public sector and the influence of the teachers union that were the main problems.

Neither the Civic Committee plan nor the mayor ever explained how starting 100 new schools would solve these problems, nor where the needed facilities would come from or where the necessary 100 highly skilled and available principals for the new schools would come from. The report reflected the Committee's bent toward vouchers but made it clear that charters would have to do until the political climate turned in a more favorable direction.

The launching of scores of new small and charter schools in Chicago cannot be understood apart from community economic redevelopment and the effort to make the city an important hub in the global economy. This objective could be met only with the reversal of white flight. In particular, Mayor Daley sought to lure back a younger version of the white middle class, the offspring of those who had fled the city forty years earlier, to escape the court-ordered integration of public schools and accommodations in the wake of the civil-rights movement.

University of Illinois at Chicago researchers David Stovall and Janet Smith summed up the Renaissance strategy this way:

> City leaders in the 1990s also began supporting initiatives to dispel the negative reputation of the Chicago Public School district by introducing charter schools, magnet schools, and privatization—all supposedly to give parents more options for their children. As a result of converging policies, many educational initiatives operate in concert with redevelopment efforts to foster displacement among the city's working-class African-American and Latino/a populations. Key to the argument for building new public schools and redeveloping public housing was that current residents would benefit. However, it can also help to attract middle-income families who might otherwise move to the suburbs or are likely to once their children reach school age.[19]

Chicago's small-schools movement was, from its inception, tied by many strings to the city's redevelopment plans and therefore represented a collage of educational and political forces, including business and educational interests—contested territory. The progressive business group, Business and Professional People for the Public Interest (BPI), led by its dynamic director, Alex Polikoff, fought to ensure that the city's destruction of high-rise public housing projects was done as fairly and humanely as possible and that new emerging communities would have mixed income housing and schools. Polikoff was the lead lawyer in the landmark 1966 Gautreaux lawsuit against the Chicago Housing Authority, resulting in a consent decree mandating more mixed-income, inner-city communities. BPI saw new "free-standing" small schools as a central component of these newly developing communities. Here's how Chicago's school-reform journal *Catalyst* described Polikoff's role and the beginnings of the city's small-school movement:

> Chicago's small-schools advocates got their inspiration in New York City, where the movement began almost 25 years ago. In 1991, Alexander Polikoff, head of Business and Professional People for the Public Interest (BPI), visited several small schools in Harlem and was won over. Soon after, BPI brought to Chicago a New York expert to meet with teachers, principals and school reform groups in Chicago. "That really kicked off the small schools effort in Chicago," Polikoff says. "We said, 'Hey, this is good stuff.' Logically, it made good sense." Polikoff then began working with University of Illinois faculty member William Ayers—his children had attended a small school in Harlem—to lead informal meetings with teachers and principals interested in setting up schools-within-schools. In 1992, Ayers, the brother of LQE's [the school reform arm of Chicago's Civic Committee] John Ayers, got a $150,000 foundation grant to open the Small Schools Workshop, a laboratory to study and create small schools in Chicago.[20]

Then there was an initial group of activist teachers trying to carve out some space for innovation and good teaching. Dozens of new schools were started. In Chicago, small elementary bilingual schools such as Telpochcalli were born. Several large, overcrowded high schools such as CVS were successfully restructured and became nationally recognized for their turnaround. New models such as a small-schools multiplex at Cregier High School emerged. Teacher-run charter schools such as Perspectives and Noble Street became laboratories of innovation and experimentation, offering new options for families.

However, under duress from the NCLB, the district pulled the rug out from under this first wave of school reform, and all traditional schools were put on a strict test-prep regimen. Across the city, principals were told to discontinue small-schools initiatives and to focus instead on test preparation. However, the small-schools movement had gone too far and attracted too much investment and popular support to turn back.

On Mothers Day, 2001, a group of parents and grandparents in Chicago's Little Village neighborhood began a hunger strike demanding that the Chicago Public Schools leadership fulfill its commitment to build a new high school in the community. Funds set aside for the new school had been spent on new selective-enrollment schools on the north side. The hunger strike drew widespread support from church and community groups, creating a political embarrassment for Mayor Daley. The hunger strikers received their victory when the new schools CEO Arne Duncan announced that the money had been "found" to build the most expensive high school in Chicago in Little Village. However, the parents didn't stop there. After much discussion and research, the community group decided that the new school for 1,450 students should be designed as a campus of four small, themed, autonomous high schools sharing a common space. They actually met regularly with the school board architects over the following year to guide the state-of-the-art design for the new school complex, which opened in the fall of 2005.

As the four new small schools at Little Village prepared to open, they were pushed to become, at least nominally, part of Renaissance 2010. However, the Little Village parents and school leaders remained outspoken in their opposition and unwilling to hand over any of their four newborn infant schools to the mayor's initiative or to accept classification under the Renaissance rubric and become either "charter," "contract," or "performance" schools.

As one of the hunger-striking mothers reminded the school board: "When we petitioned the board for years for a decent school, there was no Renaissance 2010. When we had our hunger strike, there was no Renaissance 2010. When we planned the design of the school with the architects, there was no Renaissance 2010. We aren't going to turn over our school to Renaissance 2010 now."

For many in the community, Renaissance 2010 had become a symbol of top-down, undemocratic reform, characteristic of the Ownership Society. They did not want their four new schools to be counted among the 100. Though they wanted change and risked everything to bring it about, they also wanted to keep the "public" in public schools—a theme that has been repeated in public protests across the country, from New York to New Orleans.

The first decentralizing wave of Chicago school reform was decimated by the 1995 mayoral takeover that saw many of the leaders of the small-schools movement recruited into the district administration, charter school organizations, or the foundations. Others were encouraged to become charter school operators themselves—and did.

Surviving small schools were pressured to give up many of their innovations and conform to standardized, and even scripted, modes of instruction and assessment. At one small school in particular, where the school day has been restructured to give teachers time every Friday afternoon to collaborate in their Critical Friends group, central office administrators respond each year by taking away their restructured day. Every year, the school's principal and external partners have to wage a battle to have it restored. So far, they have prevailed each year for ten years. Other successful small schools have been pressured by the big foundations to "scale up" and replicate, at a pace and scope often beyond their capacity. For most educators, just maintaining the quality level in their own small schools is a sufficiently challenging task. Getting into the replication business is something else entirely.

The Metropolitan Regional Career and Technical Center ("The MET") began in 1996 in Providence, Rhode Island as a small high school led by a couple of highly acclaimed educators, Dennis Littky and Elliott Washor. The two recruited a team of like-minded teachers, formed a nonprofit agency called the Big Picture Company, and got the state to fund a network of six small public schools spread across three local campuses. They also received support from several foundations and private supporters, including CVS drugstore chain cofounder Stanley Goldstein, who led a $20 million fund-raising effort on behalf of the schools.

The MET is distinguished by its outstanding internship program, which lies at the center of each student's individualized curriculum. The school's deep commitment to personalization is manifested in many ways. Each student has an individual faculty advisor for all four years of high school. Student, parent, and advisor all collaborate to design a learning plan that meets that child's unique needs, interests, and passions and which also incorporates the MET learning goals. Hugely successful as a college prep school, The MET saw 98 percent of its graduates accepted to college since its first class graduated in 2000.

After ten years of careful expansion, the MET reached its capacity in 2005, with just over 700 students in Providence. The original MET had opened as an alternative school with fifty ninth graders in an old downtown building. When the Gates Foundation offered Littky and Washor a large grant to open dozens of replicated schools in more than a dozen cities, they found it hard to turn down.

If opening one, or even six, small high schools in a tough Providence neighborhood were difficult, it wouldn't compare to the challenge of replication. The MET became the Big Picture Company, and three Big Picture schools opened in Chicago in 2002. Though Big Picture schools had successful starts in cities such as Oakland and Denver, CPS bureaucrats had a hard time understanding MET unorthodoxy or reconciling it with NCLB or Civic Committee standardization. The school system couldn't tolerate the non-standard curriculum and ended up undermining and then phasing the schools out despite their exceptionally high graduation rates. In Chicago neighborhoods where scarcely 30 percent of students graduate, the Big Picture Schools graduated nearly all of the members of their first class.

Many of the young teachers who started the original small-schools movement in Chicago have now left the teaching profession. The rise of the education management organizations, with their corporate professionals, has made it difficult if not impossible for small groups of teachers to create new small schools and compete for space and resources. The result is a shakeout in the industry, with the amateurs falling by the wayside as the small-schools movement morphs into a new-schools enterprise, putting the very life of school reform and public schooling at risk.

Despite everything that has been thrown against it, the small-schools movement continues to endure. It's been more than thirty years since Deborah Meier and fellow teachers opened the doors at Central Park East Elementary School in Harlem. Though there have certainly been setbacks and difficult challenges, small schools have proven themselves to be no fad. The movement has reshaped the whole way in which we now look at public education. There is hardly a school district in the United States that has not been affected. The question is no longer about the benefits of small schools. There is already an abundance of research to affirm those benefits, especially when it comes to the education of those students deepest in need. Now the question has more to do with change and transformation. How do we change a system of schooling already under attack by the forces of privatization and standardization? Read, the Ownership Society?

2

THE OWNERSHIP SOCIETY —NOT JUST A BUMPER STICKER

To give every American a stake in the promise and future of our country, we will bring the highest standards to our schools, and build an ownership society.
—President George W. Bush, Inaugural Address, 2005.

The Ownership Society has become much more than a slogan on a conservative bumper sticker. For many public education advocates and progressive educators, the slogan has come to represent an all-out assault on teachers, public schools, and public space in general. Behind it stands a new incarnation of governmental power, armed with a K–12 education law that institutionalizes and legitimizes its intervention in local school districts as never before. This intervention has little to do with the kind of federal intervention we demanded and rarely received during the school integration battles of the 1950s and

1960s. Instead, we see a new formation of neoconservative governmental power entwined with a new complex of education companies and service contractors gradually usurping public space and public decision making. As a *Wall Street Journal* writer put it: "Teachers, parents and principals may have their doubts about No Child Left Behind. But business loves it."[1]

We realized early on that real school reform and the movement for small and personalized schools could not succeed unless we confronted Ownership Society culture and politics. This was a difficult course for us and many others to take, not only because of the vindictive nature of the system of patronage that rewards, through its control over grants and contracts, obedience, loyalty, and acquiescence but because many of our colleagues are still persuaded by the rhetoric and promises of No Child Left Behind (NCLB), and we ran the risk of political isolation in a big city that often feels like a small town.

Readers may well ask, "What's so odious about ownership that you raise such a stink?" We hope this chapter provides an answer. It's not ownership we oppose but the demagogic misuse of the word to provide a rationale for the disintegration of public space in a democratic society. Demagogy has become a hallmark of the current administration. It's easy to be taken in by the rhetoric of "higher standards," leaving "no child behind," of putting "reading first." It's easy to hold onto hope for reconciliation when we hear these fine words spoken by the president. It's only natural that committed educators and public school advocates would be first in line to respond to the latest in a long line of real or fabricated crises and attacks on public education, which are used to justify every encroachment into public space and democratic decision making.[2]

We still shake our heads in disbelief when we replay Bush's speech at the 2000 National Association for the Advancement of Colored People convention—where he drew loud applause for delivering some clever speechwriter's phrase about "the soft bigotry of low expectations" and then went on to quote the ominously memorable statement by socialist intellectual and civil rights leader Dr. W.E.B. Dubois: "Either the United States will destroy ignorance or ignorance will destroy the United States." What chutzpah!

The Ownership Society has created a gloomy, crisis-laden narrative about public education, employing what Kenneth Saltman terms "the politics of disaster."[3] President Bush's sloganeering signaled an era wherein wealth and the political power it buys became concentrated in ever fewer hands, leaving more and more children behind, more and more families— 37 million, or one in eight Americans—pulled under by the riptide of poverty. All this while the top 300,000 American earners pocketed almost as much income as the bottom 150 million in 2005.

The era is marked by what one journalist called "the downsizing of America," the mass layoffs that saw hundreds of companies destroyed by short-sighted reinvestment schemes, sacrificing companies, worker skills, and economic stability for more rapid returns and a fatter bottom line for stockholders. The United States has become a debtor nation as its manufacturing jobs disappear, replaced by low-wage service and retail jobs and a permanent underclass, with the largest prison population among all industrialized nations. Unions have mainly gone the way of industrial production. The blue-collar unionization rate fell from 43.1 percent in 1978 to 19.2 percent in 2005—a drop of well over half. This has increased worker insecurity and decreased the influence and the old political base of the Democratic Party, destroying the original civil-rights–labor coalition on which the party was built and threatening to turn the Democrats into a permanent minority party.

Wal-Mart, a company that was just a small blip on the radar screen until 1980, has become the largest single employer in the United States and the leading distributor of foreign manufactured goods. It has reshaped the whole way in which we look at jobs in society and mocks the pontification to America's youth: that U.S. corporations have lots of highly skilled, high-paying jobs waiting for you if only you get an education. The Wal-Martization of America is also a planned pauperization of a large section of this country's working class. Without a plan for the redevelopment of modern industries and high-tech manufacturing in this country, it's foolish to mythologize and dangerous to tie job possibilities directly and singularly to schooling.

Corporate and government subcontracting are now key components in the Ownership Society. Ever fewer brand-named industrial firms actually make what they sell. Instead, they subcontract the work on a global scale. And subcontracting is not just about industrial production; it's become the way in which government does business (or vice-versa). Whether it's fighting a war in Iraq or operating public schools, subcontracting and the privatization of public services has created a firewall to protect an administration from public accountability, especially when it violates union contracts, environmental protection laws, or citizens' constitutional rights.

The intensified battle between the public and private spheres has deeply effected public schools, which have in turn been forced to shoulder the blame for the declining position of the United States in the world economy. The business model of management, measurement, and instruction has been forcefully driven into public school systems, especially under the punitive and test-crazy policies of the No Child Left Behind Act (NCLB). Teachers have to completely revamp methods and strategies to focus almost exclusively on test preparation. The public school curriculum has been pared down to the exclusion of nearly everything except math, science, and basic skills, especially in schools attended by children of color and kids from low-income families. Arts and critical thinking have been left behind. In some Texas districts, for example, the arts and music are being removed from course lists or being reduced to non-graded electives. The intent is to discourage students, especially high school seniors, from enrolling in art classes or pursuing electives or courses in which they might actually be interested.

"High stakes testing is the domain of the ownership society," says CUNY professor Michelle Fine. "We need real accountability. It's not about our position in global economy."[4] This statement cuts right to the heart of Ownership Society education politics, which currently drives so much of what goes on in classrooms.

Meanwhile, Secretary of Education Margaret Spellings has been out campaigning for the narrowest test-driven curriculum in our nation's history. Not an educator herself, she views education and testing through a lens of student deficits. Teaching becomes training them in a narrow group of skill sets. Differences in learning styles don't matter; neither do the varied interests of students and teachers. "There are certain things you can't teach in a classroom that our students already have—qualities like creativity, diversity, and entrepreneurship," Spellings told the audience at the 2006 National NCLB Summit. "Our job is to give them the knowledge and skills to compete."[5] However, she never explains where she thinks kids learn about diversity, creativity, and entrepreneurship, if not in school.

Spellings's version of testing is about catching kids in their ignorance rather than offering a multitude of ways for them to demonstrate what they know. It's a deficit model that runs counter to most everything we know about the differences in the ways by which individual students learn. To Spellings, testing is a high-stakes sorting game, an attempt to weed out the kids who don't necessarily do well on standardized tests. Multiple assessments—providing students with different ways to show what they know—are the enemy.

Today's neocon "radicals," such as Spellings and her predecessor, Rod Paige, hold nearly all the important positions of power and are driving their own version of reform from the top. Their top administrators move easily between department and department, agency and agency, from think tank to think tank. There is no better representative of versatility than Spellings's recently appointed assistant secretary, Williamson Evers. Evers, a Hoover Institution fellow, followed Paul Bremer to Baghdad to run the Coalition Provisional Authority's educational mission. Before that, he was a leader in the libertarian movement that invented the term *ownership society*. However, he will most likely be remembered as the ideologue that wrote polemics against the use of the phrase "social justice" in the new Iraqi constitution.[6]

They have enlisted an army of conservative think tanks, friendly corporations, and some of the biggest and most powerful philanthropists. They have used their own version of crisis and disaster politics to manipulate school reform to serve a very narrow political base. Some are even quite willing to "blow up the system" to save it, watching the old statues fall without a viable, democratic alternative. Others in the world of for-profit school management see the public education system simply as a potential profit center. All this forces us to rethink school reform strategies in a way that takes into account both the saving and the changing of public education.

From the start, Bush's education budget clearly reflected Ownership Society priorities. By his second term, public education was on the losing end of a battle for funds, with a bloated war budget more than twice the size of the K–12 education budget. Bush was pushing to eliminate forty-five federal programs that had become lifelines for reformers, including the $235 million Comprehensive School Reform Demonstration Program. The proposed 2003 and 2004 education budgets froze funding for training and retraining of teachers, even though, to Bush's credit, the NCLB mandates had significantly increased teacher academic and certification qualification requirements.

By 2000, one in five students in the United States lived in a home where a language other than English was spoken; the NCLB mandated standardized testing for English language learners. Yet, the 2003 and 2004 budgets froze program funding to support English language learners. Funding for the twenty-first century After-School Learning Centers was cut by 40 percent, eliminating programs for 563,000 latchkey children. Even the NCLB budget would be slashed by more than $200 million.

Both of Bush's education secretaries, Rod Paige and then Margaret Spellings, lobbied unsuccessfully for elimination of the Smaller Learning Communities (SLC) grants, Perkins grants for vocational and career education, and GEARUP, three federal programs at the heart of high school reform—all carryovers from previous administrations. In their place, more than $756 million in new initiatives was proposed to promote "school choice," a concept that originated with the small-schools movement but had gradually come to mean school vouchers and privatization under the new administration. Another $135 million would be allocated to support public school transfers, and $320 million would go to charter schools, much of it for privatization: a $75 million "choice incentive fund" for private school vouchers and $226 million in tuition tax credits for private schools.

Shifting budget priorities were soon being reflected in classroom practices. Recent studies, including a major one by the Rand Corporation, show sizable percentages of educators now spending more time teaching test-taking strategies, focusing more narrowly on the topics covered on state tests, and tailoring teaching to the "bubble kids"—the students who fall just below the proficiency cutoffs on state tests.[7]

Ownership Society forces have also targeted many of the hard-won gains of the civil rights era and the promise of Brown v. Board of Education. A recent Supreme Court decision, pushed by a narrow five-to-four majority of conservative justices, all but liquidated the Brown decision and codified segregated schooling when it ruled in favor of a Seattle parent who argued that school desegregation efforts that took race into account in school admissions discriminated against her white son. Behind that ruling stood the legacy of a Nixon-appointed Supreme Court Justice, a right-wing foundation, and intertwined political forces who feared school integration as an anti-business policy initiative. The late Justice Lewis Powell, before he was named to the high court, was a Virginia lawyer who wrote a memo to a friend at the U.S. Chamber of Commerce titled "Attack on the American Free Enterprise System." In the memo, Powell expressed concern that liberal groups were using specialist lawyers and developing legal strategies in support of government regulations that could limit some big business prerogatives.

Powell advocated "constant surveillance" of textbook and television content and a purge of left-wing elements. His memo would instigate a business-backed network that included several not-for-profit, conservative law firms, including the lawyers and supporters from the Pacific Legal Foundation, the very group that took the lead in prosecuting the 2007 Seattle anti-integration case. What a perfect portrait of the current assault on democratic schooling.

As benign as school reform often seems, ultimately it runs into a face-off with the cultural and business imperatives of scaling up and managing risk and of competition in the marketplace, or what University of Texas political scientist Walter Dean Burnham calls the "hegemony of market theology."

The term *ownership society* was first coined by the Cato Institute, a libertarian think tank, and specifically by the Institute's director, David Boaz, a former Bush advisor. However, the neoconservatives who took over in 2000 were neither libertarians nor traditional, pro-business, anti-regulation conservatives, and the Cato people probably rue the day they handed them that clever slogan.

Most people think of neoconservatism and neoliberalism as ideologies favoring smaller government and freer markets. When it comes to schools, the word *vouchers* probably comes to mind. However, the neoconservatives who took over the White House and the Department of Education in 2001 were hardly interested in smaller government or, for that matter, even in vouchers. Unlike their anti-government forebears who wanted to "blow up" the Department of Education, minimize the federal role in public education, and institute a national voucher program, this new breed of conservatives dreamed of a fatter Department of Education, more influence in local schools, and greater control over a huge federal K–12 budget that could be leveraged against any political opposition.

They took the ownership society slogan from Boaz and ran with it. They elevated the expropriation of language to an art form, taking Marian Wright Edelman's enduring phrase, "leave no child behind"—the watchword of the Children's Defense Fund—and turning it into their own mantra for standardized testing. They used the same alchemy on our small-schools movement, taking our anti-bureaucracy concepts such as school choice and autonomy and deforming them into code for school closings, privatization, and union busting.

The ownership society terminology has also been credited to such futurist paradigm-shifters as Peter Drucker and Alvin Toffler and to the late free-market economist Milton Friedman. However, its philosophical underpinnings extend back to Aristotle who, in his critique of Plato's constitution, wrote, "What belongs in common to the most people, is accorded the least care. They take thought for their own things above all, and less about things common."

Aristotle considered the crowd to be given to evil and saw common things being less loved by most people and consequently less cared for than those things that are their own. Among such people, he said, the appropriation of things is better than community.

The notion that the welfare of individuals is directly related to their ability to control their own lives and wealth, rather than to government benevolence, is a longstanding one, usually associated with "Reaganomics" and British conservatism (especially Thatcherism), but also expounded by 1960s student activists such as SDS leader Tom Hayden, who wrote about the ideals of participatory democracy in the 1962 manifesto, "The Port Huron Statement":

> Some would have us believe that Americans feel contentment amidst prosperity—but might it not better be called a glaze above deeply felt anxieties about their role in the new world? And if these anxieties produce a developed indifference to human affairs, do they not as well produce a yearning to believe there is an alternative to the present, that something can be done to change circumstances in the school, the workplaces, the bureaucracies, the government?[8]

This statement could easily have been included in any early mission statement of the small-schools movement as well, a movement that developed in urban school districts a quarter century later. We've traveled a long way from participatory democracy to the Ownership Society. Both phrases signify watershed moments in American history. Each shaped the way whereby we looked at our lives, our values, our schools, and our government.

Turning points in national educational policy have often been marked by such slogans and by wars, social movements, legislative acts, or bully-pulpit speeches. Franklin Roosevelt had his "New Deal" and Lyndon Johnson, his "Great Society." Richard

Nixon called for "a New American Revolution," and Bill Clinton invoked a "New Covenant." Usually, in times of war—hot or cold—new language is created to set the table for the shift away from policies or projects that encourage or fund educational progressivism. A new national education agenda focused on science and mathematics for war production, industrial development, making the country more competitive with its European or Asian rivals, or other perceived national political priorities goes into full swing and supersedes local policies or initiatives. This shift is usually accompanied by warnings of impending doom and disaster if the new policies (usually wars) against drugs or terrorism are not immediately implemented. We can point to Newt Gingrich's testimony before the Senate Committee on Commerce, Science and Transportation, when he called U.S. public education's inability to refocus its curriculum on math and science the second greatest threat to America, adding, "only the threat of a weapon of mass destruction in an American city [is] a greater danger."[9]

The Soviet launch of Sputnik also launched the Defense Education Act in 1958 and the era of the large, comprehensive high school. It was a jumping off point for James Bryant Conant's 1959 book, *The American High School Today*.[10] Conant's study put the national spotlight on secondary education much as the small-schools movement has done today. He envisioned the twentith-century high school as an egalitarian, democratic place, serving an increasingly diverse student body with literally hundreds of courses that prepared some for college and others for stable jobs in the booming postwar industrial economy. However, his work also led to bigger and more heavily tracked high schools.

Conant, though liberal in many respects, would have been a prototype Ownership Society thinker, floating easily between the military and education sides of government. His view of the American high schools was filtered as much through the lens of the Cold War as through that of educational research. He was a chemical and biological weapons expert, an advisor for the Atomic Energy Commission, and the president of Harvard University as well as being a public education consultant-reformer. Though some current DOE leaders migrated from the war rooms, no one in the current administration even approaches the stature of Conant as an intellectual giant in his time.

World War II had put an end to one of the most important experiments in American education with the close, in 1940, of the Progressive Education Association's Eight-Year Study.[11] The study was intended to determine whether students educated in small, progressive schools, alternatives to the traditional models, could be successful college students. In fact, they did better in both academic and nonacademic areas. By demonstrating that student success could be measured and predicted in a variety of ways, the study encouraged a transformation in educational evaluation procedures, making them more democratic. However, by 1940, the political agenda of the country shifted, and schools were put on a war footing. The findings and impact of the Eight-Year Study were muted once again, by a crisis that confronted the nation.

On rare occasions, such historic turning points have been for the better, coming in response to real, rather than manufactured, crises and to pressures from progressive social movements, which drove positive reforms such as school desegregation in the 1950s. However, more often, the opposite has held true. The 1983 report, "A Nation at Risk,"[12] is often cited as the founding or watershed document of modern-day school reform. In many respects it was just that, a shining of the national spotlight on the so-called failures of public education. However, "A Nation at Risk" predated the sense of alarm and the mentality of perpetual crisis all too familiar to us now in the post-9/11 Ownership Society:

> If an unfriendly power had attempted to impose on America the mediocre educational performance that exists today, we might well have viewed it as an act of war. As it stands, we have allowed this to happen to ourselves. We have even squandered the gains in achievement made in the wake of the Sputnik challenge. Moreover, we have dismantled essential support systems, which helped make those gains possible. We have, in effect, been committing an act of unthinking, unilateral educational disarmament.

This tactic, in which some unnamed or vague external enemy is ready to "follow us home" from Russia, China, or the Middle East or to outmaneuver us in the space race or in the race for economic supremacy, is now a featured argument in nearly every new commission report on public education. It equates the failures of public education, real or exaggerated, as the work of traitors to the national interest. It's an easy way of playing on flag-waving nationalism, especially in time of war, to force new top-down reforms on the public. The most recent example was the 2006 report of the New Commission on Skills of the American Workforce, "Tough Choices or Tough Times."[13] This commission repeats an earlier warning that globalization is "creating a world in which there would be less and less room… for people with relatively low skills." Despite the dire warning, the Commission offers neither real programs nor strategies for giving children of color or those from poor families access to the kind of teaching that will get them recognition in the globalized world. Cities such as New York, London, Paris, Hong Kong, and Moscow are increasingly becoming unaffordable and unlivable if you aren't a multi-millionaire.

The renewed sense of national urgency about schooling is absolutely legitimate. Generations of young people are being denied the basic instruments of economic opportunity. No doubt the workforce of the present and the future are being severely maimed. However, the politics of disaster has been used to make the case for a top-down orientation, standardization, and re-centralization not limited to the education arena but extending to all areas of civic life and government. The politics of disaster serve the Bush administration as the pretext, justifying the abrogation of a range of civil liberties and constitutional guarantees right up to such basic elements as habeas corpus. It was in this spirit of national emergency and fear that the Social Security system was collapsing that President Bush first used the term *Ownership Society* in a February, 2003 speech in Kennesaw, Georgia. It was a pivotal moment in the period between 9/11 and the actual start of the war in Iraq, though little heralded at the time. Bush said: "I think all public policy, or as much public policy as possible, ought to encourage people to own something." The more people own, the President reasoned, "the more they'll have a stake in the future of this country." And when Bush said "all" public policy, he meant all.

That speech ushered in what Paul Krugman of the *New York Times* would call "the new gilded age," an era wherein nearly all new federal initiatives, whether in war planning, tax incentives, health, or education policy, were aimed at transferring as much wealth and power as possible away from the public sector and into the private.

The four years following 9/11 would represent the largest shift of wealth and power in this country's history, with concentrations of personal and corporate wealth not seen since the 1920s. Bill Moyers described the period as the moment in U.S. history in which a "shining city on the hill" morphed into a "gated community whose privileged occupants, surrounded by a moat of money and protected by a political system seduced with cash into subservience, are removed from the common life of the country."

Conjuring up his own images of an invasion of America, Moyers added:

Inspired by bumper-sticker abstractions of Milton Friedman's ideas, propelled by cascades of cash from corporate chieftains like Coors and Koch and 'Neutron' Jack Welch, fortified by the pious prescriptions of fundamentalist political preachers like Jerry Falwell and Pat Robertson, the conservative armies marched on Washington. And they succeeded brilliantly.[14]

Unfettered by any reasonable standards of fairness or commonality, a manager of a hedge fund could now take home more than $1.2 billion in salary, while the top twenty-five managers combined made about $14 billion. That, by the way, matches the combined annual budgets of New York and Chicago's public school systems and equals the cost of providing health care for a year to 8 million children—the approximate number of children in this country who do not at present have health insurance.

The Ownership Society has spawned its own literature, including a genre of self-help books, of which the most successful is Rhonda Byrne's *The Secret*, the quintessential paean to personal wealth cultivation and new-age problem solving through belief in the great individual, rather than through social action. *The Secret* promotes the "Law of Attraction"—that as a man (or woman) thinketh, so shall he or she be. Only great, rich, successful, and powerful individuals, such as Citigroup's Sanford Weill, or Bill Gates, Michael Bloomberg, and Oprah Winfrey really know The Secret and can solve problems that the rest of us can't, because they have the innate capacity to visualize success. That is why they are successful.

There is no problem—a slumping stock market, school reform, the war against terrorism, or gathering personal wealth and power—that can't be solved, if we only leave it in their hands. Perhaps the success of books such as *The Secret* are the result of aggressive marketing techniques. Another possible explanation for their popularity lies in the desperation that people feel when faced with challenges that appear unsolvable to the ordinary citizen—problems that seem too complex for ordinary citizens to get their hands around.

We hunger for answers, but how can we make decisions about war and peace, or how to create good schools for our children, when we don't have access to the "secret" intelligence data? How can we know how to solve the perennial problems of public education unless there are clear and discernible metrics that tell us what a good school is? That is the great advantage the top-down model of change favored over the more democratic, participatory model. We want to believe that great men and women already have answers and that the answers are simple if you have the technology at your service, and know the secret.

There are, of course, the Ownership Society contrarians. Both James Sinegal, chief executive of Costco, and venture billionaire Warren Buffett argue that the current system, which concentrates so much wealth at the top, is obscene.

The first target of the Ownership Society was the Social Security system, the bedrock of the New Deal, first signed into law by President Franklin D. Roosevelt in 1935 in the wake of the Great Depression. By invoking the same crisis consciousness that provides much of the rationale for its other "radical" reforms, the Bush administration insisted that the traditional Social Security program was going broke and should be largely replaced with private retirement accounts.

As for public health care, the current administration seems to share an attitude with the legendary French aristocrat who, on hearing that the peasants had no bread, advised, "Let them eat cake." Responding to the growing health care crisis, with the exclusion of more than 40 million Americans from the health insurance system, Paul Krugman, noting Bush's cavalier attitude toward the health care crisis, reported that the President told a crowd in July, 2007, "I mean, people have access to health care in America…After all, you just go to an emergency room." One can only imagine the chaos that would ensue if the 40 million Americans presently excluded from the health insurance system each took Bush's advice and presented themselves at their local emergency room (Krugman, July 16, 2007).

Taxation became far less progressive under the Ownership Society, building on a trend that has been developing since the 1970s, of taxing dividends and capital gains at a lower rate, 15 percent, than that assessed on the earned income of most middle-class families. The estate tax was phased out, and any talk of shoring up Social Security through increased corporate or payroll taxes was taken off the table. Privatization was the one note the Republican administration could play.

Once again, using the threat of imminent disaster and the climate of fear after 9/11, and even taking advantage of the national catastrophe that was Hurricane Katrina, Ownership Society interests moved quickly and powerfully, using every force at their disposal, from a bribed section of the media to a cadre of self-interested think tanks and philanthropists, to help to create a favorable climate for the shift in the whole structure of public education.

The Department of Education stuffed $240,000 into the pocket of journalist and former Clarence Thomas aide Armstrong Williams in exchange for his favorable coverage of the NCLB and his attacks on the National Education Association and as payola for interviewing Education Secretary Rod Paige. More insidious was the direct funding of articles in *Education Week* by increasingly politicized and self-interested foundations. A case can be made for foundations providing funding for education journals. However, when the funders underwrite articles that turn out to be puff pieces about those very foundations or directly fund articles that one-sidedly reflect the Ownership Society perspective on school reform, questions of conflict of interests are bound to arise.

Hurricane Katrina for example, was used as a rationale to use federal emergency relief money for the creation of privately managed charter schools. In the nation's capitol, a public school system long ravaged by a man-made disaster of mismanagement and neglect was used as a rationale for subcontracting or selling off schools to a flock of high-paid, politically connected consulting companies, vividly described by a *Washington Post* reporter:

> Two dozen high-priced consultants have set up shop on three floors of the D.C. public schools' headquarters, wearing pinstripe suits, toting binders and Blackberrys and using such corporate jargon as "resource mapping" and "identifying metrics." They come from big-name restructuring firms, and the city is paying $4 million for their services this summer. The findings of the consultants...could have a large bearing on whether his [Mayor Fenty's] plan to overhaul the troubled 55,000-student system is successful.[15]

For decades, D.C. schools have been largely run by consulting teams from companies such as McKinsey, Alvarez & Marsal, and KMPG without any measurable improvement, either on the organizational or instructional side. Urban superintendents (or CEOs as they are now called) have been virtually turned into highly paid procurement officers. The parade of powerhouse consultants continues from D.C. to St. Louis, with politically connected school superintendents, consultants, and foundation officers moving freely from one consulting job to the other, through all of these institutions, working both sides of the street. The size of contracts and the scope of school district subcontracting have never been greater than it is under the Ownership Society.

Emerging from the Cold War era, conservative theorists led by Milton Friedman bashed the idea of "government schools" and used their Cold War critique of "collectivism" to promote unfettered capitalism as the natural order. Privatization and school voucher initiatives were hailed as the most effective ways to manage and market schools. Conservatives viewed education as just another purchasable commodity. Schools, like supermarkets or restaurants, were seen as enterprises better run directly by private companies, competing for a consumer dollar, bolstered by government vouchers.

To shore up this pursuit, voucher advocate Herbert Walberg of the University of Illinois at Chicago went so far as to deny the existence of "capitalism." He and other traditional conservatives had always considered capitalism as an economic system growing from nature itself, the natural way for all humans to live. Quoting Thomas Sowell, another conservative pundit, Walberg wrote,

> Since capitalism was named by its enemies...it is perhaps not surprising that the name is completely misleading. Despite the name, capitalism is not an "ism." It is not a philosophy but an economy. Ultimately it is nothing more and nothing less than an economy not run by political authorities.[16]

Libertarians and free-market-eers must have been taken aback by the new Ownership Society model that, while certainly the embodiment of capitalism, had less to do with free markets than it did with bigger government serving as a conduit for public funding of private enterprise and most certainly run by "political authorities."

Conservative economist Stephen Moore provided the first comprehensive analysis of George Bush's second-term agenda of creating a "broad-based ownership society."[17] Moore glowingly describes a future in which Americans would have a bigger stake in the American economy in the next Bush administration. Moore, the president of the influential Club for Growth, writes:

The Clinton recession has been converted into the Bush boom...The central insight behind this idea of letting every American own a piece of the rock, to borrow from the advertising phrase, is that expanding personal ownership of the nation's resources is the antidote to big government...As more Americans become genuine capitalists their wealth comes from what they own, not what the government gives them.

The impact of the Ownership Society has been felt in all domains of social and public policy, from welfare reform to infrastructure development, in tax policy, housing, and health and retirement plans, and even in student loans. What better way for ordinary citizens to own a piece of the rock than by government using public funds to subsidize banks, other lending organizations, and large developers with the so-called American Dream Down Payment Assistance Act, which was signed into law in December of 2003 This law allowed people who earn less than 80 percent of the median income in a region, in a city, or in a locality to get a government-sponsored down payment, 10 percent of the value of the house—or $10,000, to help them purchase their first home. Four years later, thousands of these homes were being repossessed as the housing market collapsed owing largely to sub-prime loan lending to borrowers who couldn't afford the bill that would come due.

As far as health care was concerned, Democratic Congresswoman Gwen Moore of Milwaukee put it this way: "Bush has often pushed for an ownership society in America. His health care proposal is yet another example of what he means by that: You're on your own."[18]

There's probably no better example of the Ownership Society's erosion of public space than the 2007 sale of Sallie Mae, the nation's largest student loan firm, to a huge banking consortium spearheaded by J.P. Morgan/Chase and Bank of America, at the highest price ever paid for a financial company:

$25 billion. Until 1997, Sallie Mae was a public agency with a public mission—to make low-interest loans to college students. As tuitions rose, rendering a university degree all but inaccessible to millions of students from middle- and low-income families, potential profits skyrocketed. The privatized Sallie Mae thrived with federal subsidies and guarantees. The sale of Sallie Mae brought with it grave concern that its public mission would be eradicated in an industry already plagued by kickback scandals and unlawful access to student databases, which, in the student loan industry, amount to an unfair advantage paralleling insider stock tips. To a public agency, the well-being and education of the students is supposed to trump profits.

As matters progressed, it became increasingly apparent that the Ownership Society was less about individual ownership than it was about a strengthened government–corporate "partnership" that could funnel public dollars to a relatively few politically aligned companies. It would mean selling off public space, public services, prisons, and even military services to consortia of private investors. This power shift shrank the political base of the Democratic Party, particularly its labor union base. Schools, hospitals, even public highways and thoroughfares—no area of public space was immune to what was popularly termed *restructuring*. Indiana, for example, handed over the operation of the 157-mile Indiana Toll Road to a foreign-owned consortium, which paid $3.8 billion for a seventy-five-year lease on this major highway.

Chicago Mayor Richard Daley, a Democrat who often expressed admiration for George Bush, easily transitioned into Ownership Society politics when it came to public education, government patronage, and urban redevelopment strategies, even selling off the famed Chicago Skyway for $1.8 billion. His education reform plan was shaped, in large measure, by the Commercial Club of Chicago and its public policy arm, the Civic Committee. This elite network of the most powerful and influential sector of the business community has the mayor's ear on all major policy issues. In recent years, the Civic Committee has been the loudest critic of the "public school monopoly" and of the Chicago Teachers Union.

Following Daley's lead in taking direct control of public schools, other big-city mayors from Baltimore to Los Angeles caught Ownership Society fever, focusing privatization efforts on the management of many city systems and institutions, most notably the public school system. The Senate began hearings on "public–private partnerships," an increasingly popular financing model that became a hallmark of the Ownership Society. Cash-strapped state and local governments invited the private sector to lease existing public facilities and to develop or operate new ones (or do both). However, John J. Duncan, Jr., the Tennessee Republican, ominously warned that while state governments may secure large up-front payments for privatizing their roads, they could leave future generations "holding the bag."

Duncan described "sweetheart deals" for private companies. While technically renting the roads, the leasing companies can extend the length of the leases—which can extend for up to ninety-nine years—to depreciate their value as if they actually owned the roads. This, in turn, can translate to tens, even hundreds of millions of dollars in tax breaks.[19]

However, Congressman Duncan's concern was too little and too late. The Ownership cow was well out of the barn. Like the Gold Rush of 1849, the great sell-off of the country's economic infrastructure had begun. Today's '49ers are the privatizers of the New Millennium, panning for gold in the public revenue stream. The selling off of the intellectual infrastructure would soon follow.

The events of 9/11 gave impetus to the Ownership Society's move toward a new form of government partnership with the private sector in its response to the threat of terrorism. This highly portable partnership could easily be carried over from the Pentagon to the Department of Education. The No Child Left Behind Act of 2001 included the provision that school districts that receive federal funds must provide military recruiters with high school student contact information. The DOE came to rival the Department of Defense (DOD) as a profit source for private contractors and an ideological support for the Ownership Society. The half-trillion dollars spent annually on public education roughly equaled the dollar amount spent on the war in Iraq.

Some time after September 11, 2001, Christopher Whittle, the founder of Edison Schools, Inc., one of the biggest beneficiaries of administration largesse, described his vision of a new American system of education, based on alliances between the federal government and for-profit companies. In his dream, the partnerships would rival those over at the Department of Defense. In his 2005 book, *Crash Course*, Whittle calls for a new wave of federal legislation to defend and consolidate the states' charter school laws and funnel billions of federal dollars to private providers of services and supports. Writes Whittle,

> This legislation will be timely because today, unlike 15 years ago, serious private-sector education partners can be called upon by the federal government. While two decades ago the feds would have had almost nowhere to turn for assistance in the creation and launch of new schools in America, now they have perhaps a dozen entities that could be both designers and providers. They include players like Sylvan, Edison Schools, National Heritage Academies, the University of Phoenix, DeVry, the Broad Foundation, and the Gates Foundation. And if presented with the right opportunities, the entrepreneurs at companies not directly included in school management, such as McGraw-Hill and Pearson, might engage as well.

Whittle's list of "serious private-sector education partners" reads like a Who's Who of the Ownership Society, a list Whittle himself probably wouldn't have made unless he had drawn it up. McGraw-Hill, for example, already was "engaged." The giant textbook company is one of the biggest suppliers of reading instructional materials approved under the DOE's Reading First program and by the National Reading Panel's "scientifically based" standards of excellence. The company has used its connections to great advantage in the highly competitive K–12 textbook publishing field, in which just three companies conduct 85 percent of all textbook sales business. A group of McGraw-Hill authors dominated Governor George W. Bush's Texas reading advisory board. Open Court, one of McGraw-Hill's reading textbook series, became Bush's, and then-Houston Superintendent Rod Paige's, program of choice. Harold McGraw, the publishing scion and chairman of McGraw-Hill, is one of Bush's closest personal friends.

Nation writer Stephen Metcalf connects the reading dots:

Harold McGraw Jr. sits on the national grant advisory and founding board of the Barbara Bush Foundation for Family Literacy. McGraw in turn received the highest literacy award from President Bush in the early 1990s, for his contributions to the cause of literacy. The McGraw Foundation awarded ... Bush Education Secretary Rod Paige its highest educator's award while Paige was Houston's school chief; Paige, in turn, was the keynote speaker at McGraw-Hill's "government initiatives" conference...Harold McGraw III was selected as a member of President George W. Bush's transition advisory team, along with McGraw-Hill board member Edward Rust Jr., the CEO of State Farm and an active member of the Business Roundtable on educational issues. An ex-chief of staff for Barbara Bush is returning to work for Laura Bush in the White House—after a stint with McGraw-Hill as a media relations executive. John Negroponte left his position as McGraw-Hill's executive vice president for global markets to become Bush's ambassador to the United Nations. And over the years, Bush's education policies have been a considerable boon to the textbook publishing conglomerate.[20]

McGraw-Hill's Negroponte would later become U.S. Ambassador to the U.N., Ambassador to Iraq, Bush's first Director of National Intelligence (overseeing spying, not reading instruction), and then Deputy Secretary of State.

The events of 9/11 gave renewed momentum to the Ownership Society's all-encompassing drive toward privatization, especially to private management of public space, in its response to the threat of terrorism. Jeremy Scahill documents this in his book, *Blackwater: The Rise of the World's Most Powerful Mercenary Army*. Scahill sees a much larger hand operating here than simply that of the military:

> The Bush administration came to power with the most radical privatization agenda in U.S. history, and we see it in our schools, we see it in prisons, we see it in healthcare, we see it in local law enforcement in the United States, federal law enforcement as well. And now with the so-called war on terror and the occupation of Iraq, we've seen the most militant privatization agenda sort of unfold before our eyes. Donald Rumsfeld, on September 10th, 2001, gave one of his first major addresses at the Pentagon, and he laid out a plan for a wholesale sort of overhaul of how the U.S. would wage its wars. And he talked about a small-footprint approach and the use of the private sector, and at one point Rumsfeld said because governments can't die, we need to find other incentives for bureaucracy to adapt and improve. And of course this was one day before this sort of new Pearl Harbor moment happened on September 11th and all of a sudden Rumsfeld and Cheney get this blank canvas on which to paint their privatization dreams.[21]

On the education front, conservative journalists began timing their columns and commentaries to mesh with new initiatives coming out of Education Secretary Rod Paige's (and later Margaret Spellings's) Department of Education. Their messages had a familiar ring: Public education is a moribund, bureaucratic, collectivist, socialistic "monopoly" that must be replaced by a shift to privatized management of public schools and school districts.

Paige made his and the administration's attitude toward teachers and their unions very clear in his 2004 speech to the National Governors Association in which he referred to the NEA as "terrorists." Paige rekindled union bashing in his book, *The War against Hope.*[22] If someone began an argument with the words, "I have no problem with… [insert, say, Mexicans, Jews, or black people], but…" the astute listener would immediately assume that the speaker did indeed have a problem. So when Paige begins his polemic against the NEA with the words, "No, I have no problem with teachers…" but "unions represent the most imposing barrier to authentic school reform that reformers face today," right away one suspects that he (and the administration that he leads) has big problems with teachers, as well as being off kilter in his hatred of their organizations.[23]

The transformation was complete. The Ownership Society and its political leaders were now the new radicals, impatiently waiting to "blow up" the system from within and to destroy the unions, whereas progressives were considered to be gradualists, dependent on the bureaucracy for any real change, or flat-out defenders of the status quo. The 1960s were definitely dead.

Yet for many traditional conservatives, the Ownership Society was a big disappointment, as it signaled the creation of the largest and most centralized federal bureaucracy ever, with huge expenditures and a war budget surpassing the collective capacity not only of the huge Gates Foundation but the combined assets of every private foundation in the world as well.

Traditional conservatives were also critical of the neo-cons for their approach to school reform and the NCLB Act. They felt as if the neo-cons were reverting to the idea of "government schools" and a large apparatus at the DOE to support them. Conservative writer Terence Jeffrey wrote,

> President Bush has become, quite rightly, an evangelist for the virtues of private property, speaking about an "ownership society" just about everywhere he goes. Just about everywhere, that is, except when he visits a government-owned school. Then he is a big-government man.[24]

Jeffrey and other traditional conservatives believed that the NCLB diverted the movement away from vouchers, which could be used to pay for private and parochial schooling.

The Ownership Society slogan, however, had a shorter shelf life than a gallon of buttermilk on a hot August day. By January of 2006, with the election of a Democratic majority in Congress, the Ownership Society was officially declared dead. *Money* magazine's senior editor Pat Regnier wrote in its obituary:

> As the new Congress takes over, for the first time in 12 years Democratic legislators have a chance to set the agenda, and the Anxiety Economy is going to be near the top. George W. Bush's entrepreneurial, it's-your-money Ownership Society is out. What's in: addressing risk.

By March of 2007, Brendan Murray, who once described the Ownership Society as "the glue that bound together Bush's domestic agenda," was also writing the slogan's epitaph:

> The president's sales pitch for the ownership concept is being dialed back as housing prices fall, foreclosures reach record levels and U.S. stock markets shed more than $700 billion in market value over the past month. Bush, who mentioned the term three dozen times in 2004, has mentioned it only once this year.[25]

However, even as the slogan was consigned to cold storage, it had already succeeded in launching a broad range of policies and strategies that would set the stage for a major alteration in the way we conceive of public space, embracing everything from mass media to public education. It also sent a signal to corporate friends of the administration's educational policies that the new gold rush of the twenty-first century was on and, despite the rhetoric of the NCLB, lots of non-owners, small owners, or politically unreliable owners would be left behind.

As war profiteers such as Halliburton and Blackwater cashed in on the Ownership Society gravy train, a handful of well-connected publishers, school operators and service providers were also living large on such government programs as the multi-billion dollar Reading First initiative, which would come under Justice Department scrutiny by the spring of 2007, shortly after the new Congress was sworn in (April 2007).

Among those living it up was Randy Best, a Texas businessman and Bush fundraising "Pioneer" (an honorific reserved for those who raise $100,000 for the presidential campaign). Best owned Voyager Expanded Learning, a reading program that was valued at around $5 million a few years before it was awarded DOE contracts under Reading First. After the contract awards, Best was able to sell his company for $360 million.

This mythic tradition of the middle-class investor clashed with hard realities after the 2004 election. Marie Cocco at the *Washington Post* summed it up this way:

> The Ownership Society philosophy as part of Karl Rove's election strategy was meant to swing middle-class voters away from the Democratic Party. As such, the strategy has come under attack from Democratic leaders including Barack Obama and Hillary Clinton; however, with a slightly different twist, it is a philosophy, which can be embraced by Democrats as well as Republicans. For example, Robert Reich, who served as Bill Clinton's Secretary of Labor, in his

critique of Bush's ownership-society speech, retorted: "I'm all in favor of a real Ownership Society. But that's not at all what Republicans are selling."[26]

The Cato Institute's David Boaz, borrowing again from Aristotle, argues that private ownership is superior to social ownership as a rule and that people "take better care of things they own," as if selling off major institutions of civil society were comparable to teaching a kid not to leave his bike out in the rain. According to Boaz and the libertarians, private ownership solves all problems in society, from saving the environment to combating the undemocratic nature of government bureaucracy. Here, Cato really zooms in on education as the fulcrum for wider "ownership."

Echoing Friedman's philosophy on education, Cato advocates the all-out privatization of public education and the implementation of school vouchers on a broad scale—nationwide. Boaz makes his case in a Cato tract called "Why is school choice part of an ownership society?"[27] Here he makes his core argument:

> Education is of course a vital part of childhood. Parents who lack control over where their children attend school in effect cede to government ownership of the children themselves. Parental control of education, then, is an essential component of an ownership society.
>
> When parents are able to choose a school for their child, they're empowered. They've taken personal responsibility for their own child's education. But when children are assigned to a government school, parents lose this sense of ownership and responsibility. In today's society, public schools tend to be most effective in areas with high property values. Therefore, only parents who can afford to live in desirable neighborhoods or pay tuition to private schools can exert significant control over their children's education. School choice extends this control to lower- and middle-income parents as well.

Boaz claims as well that privatized schools "empower" teachers as opposed to stifling them in "government schools":

> School choice also empowers teachers, whose methods and practices are currently limited by government school regulations and curriculum. Private schools can accommodate a wide range of teaching styles and interests, and are much more flexible with certification requirements. In an ownership society, teachers could even open their own private schools, and offer their services to the public in a way that competes with the public schools. Teachers who own their schools invest more those schools' success than teachers who work for state-run schools. Private schools can also better reward talented, hard-working teachers with higher pay.

Conservative commentator Paul Glastris, writing in the *Washington Monthly*, explained their strategic thinking in embracing Friedman:

> Giving individuals more choice, control, and "ownership" of their government benefits, they argued, would not only enhance virtues like personal responsibility, but over time, it would also result in the shift of hundreds of billions of tax dollars from the custodial care of government to the corporations that would help manage people's private accounts.
>
> Best of all, from the conservative point of view, it would transform the electorate's political identity. Instead of government-dependent supporters of the Democratic Party, voters would become self-reliant followers of the GOP.[28]

Bush had this give-and-take with journalist Gwen Ifill on the "Jim Lehrer Newshour" (December 12, 2004) in which Ifill credited Bush and Vice President Cheney with the Ownership Society terminology:

Gwen Ifill: During the campaign, President Bush and Vice President Cheney coined a new phrase to describe the economic promise of a second term. They said they would create an "ownership society," one that would lower taxes and shift more of government's burden to individuals.

President Bush: I believe our country can and must become an ownership society. When you own something, you care about it. When you own something, you have a vital stake in the future of your country.

Bush was also assuring his relatively small but single-minded conservative base that free-market reforms would be pushed aggressively in the 2004 election campaign and, indeed, that the Ownership Society theme itself could become a wedge issue that would rally the troops, leaving Democrats divided and bewildered. Republican strategists were infatuated by talk of the "investor vote." They hammered at this theme for the remaining eight months of the campaign, and one could argue that it enjoyed limited success. However, the Ownership philosophy would prove to be hardly a free-market reform. Instead, it resembled something more akin to state monopoly capitalism. There was a distinct (and for neo-cons, uncomfortable) whiff of the Kremlin in the air, with the drive for bigger government, more centralization, more controls, to facilitate "ownership."

Most of Bush's speech, including his promises of $1.8 billion for matching contributions to poor peoples' saving accounts (at least, for the few who had one) was simple political smoke. More smoke was blown by those in Congress who proposed some $40 billion more for "birth accounts" or "baby bonds" for every child born in this country. In subsequent years, Congress became polarized and paralyzed by partisan infighting. The seemingly interminable "war on terror" sucked up hundreds of billions of dollars each year and pushed the country into a sinkhole of debt. Republican ownership-society initiatives such as the privatization of Social Security were dead in the water. The education "industry," conversely, represents the second largest sector of the nation's gross national product, second only to health care. In his 2003 book, *Managing in the Next Society*, the late management theorist and consultant, Peter Drucker, pointed out that "health care and education together will be 40 percent of the gross national product within 20 years. Already they are at least a third."[29] Drucker described a future in which health care and education are "outsourced."

Though both parties voted for the NCLB Act, in the context of the Republican strategy, the NCLB provided bureaucratic leverage sufficient to push students and parents from "failing" local schools into religious, private, virtual, or privately managed ones. That shift offered an avenue to reroute the flow of public dollars through vouchers. This flow would also encourage and even finance the birth and sustenance of new businesses, especially of educational management organizations (EMOs), for-profit firms established to operate the "failing" urban schools or to start new charter schools.

However, by the time the NCLB bill made it through the committee process, it had been stripped of its voucher provisions to garner enough bipartisan support for passage. "Conservatives were crestfallen, but the White House couldn't care less," moaned Ryan Sager in the conservative journal *Reason*:

> supporters of school choice should have done more to lobby lawmakers instead of expecting the White House to do it. The aide said the [voucher] issue was "never central to the president." What was central to the president was changing the politics of the education issue from favoring the Democrats overwhelmingly to favoring the Republicans at least narrowly.[30]

However, if the NCLB Act were more about political expediency than about vouchers, how would it play out for the conservatives in the face of public school realities? A study of educational management organizations by an Arizona State University research group identified between fifty and sixty for-profit EMOs operating in twenty-nine states in the wake of Bush's Ownership Society speech.[31] The NCLB would indeed give birth to many such enterprises. The report indicated a trend of outsourcing and consolidation, with the industry shaking out, leaving fewer and bigger companies managing more schools in more districts. The report also showed EMOs moving beyond direct school management and into specialty services, such as operating summer schools, providing test score analysis, after-school tutoring, test preparation, and advising schools and districts on ways to ensure compliance with the NCLB requirements for "adequate yearly progress." Schools managed by private companies, the report revealed, tended to be larger, a trend that runs counter to contemporary knowledge about school size and school improvement.

Another study, by University of Wisconsin researcher Patricia Burch,[32] identified three distinct shifts in content and structure of relationships between educational suppliers and local school districts. These were (1) elevation of test-related services and products, (2) heightened emphasis on technology-based solutions, and (3) an expanding role for the state in spurring market activity. That last shift must send shivers down the spines of traditional conservatives.

Barack Obama used the bully pulpit of his campaign to attack the Ownership Society. In a speech leading up to the 2006 midterm elections, Obama was on the stump for local Democrats. He told a cheering crowd, "There is a collective spirit that says our possibilities are boundless." But, he cautioned, "it seems as if we have an administration that believes in an ownership society ... instead of believing we're all in it together, you're on your own."[33]

Hillary Clinton took her own digs at the Ownership Society philosophy, juxtaposing it to her favorite metaphor of the "village" to talk about health care. Clinton said,

> The Bush "ownership society" applied to health care is taking the form of high-deductible "catastrophic" insurance policies, with consumers paying out of pocket and enjoying tax-free savings if they keep expenses under the deductible. This approach would make perfect sense if health care were really like frankfurters or Fords. I would argue, however, that it's not.[34]

In one of the most compelling critiques, *Columbia Journalism Review* publisher Evan Cornog blamed the cultural shift inspired by the Ownership Society for the erosion of social consciousness that was killing the traditional news media and threatening the social content of public education.[35] In a January 2005 essay Cornog wrote,

> When George W. Bush, at his party's 2004 convention, laid out his vision of America's future, it was of an "ownership society," where people would not only own their own homes but also "own their own health plans and have the confidence of owning a piece of their retirement." This "ownership society" is many things, and one of them is a premeditated privatization of responsibilities that government had taken on during the New Deal and Great Society epochs.

Larry Cuban of Stanford University blamed "business-inspired reform coalitions" for recasting public education:

> In doing so, the traditional and primary collective goal of public schools building literate citizens able to engage in democratic practices has been replaced by the goal of social efficiency, that is, preparing students for a competitive labor market anchored in a swiftly changing economy.[36]

Cuban's book, *The Blackboard and the Bottom Line: Why Schools Can't Be Businesses*, traced the rise of the social efficiency model over the last three decades. Though those economic threats have nearly evaporated, the prescription arrived at— more standardized tests of basic skills, and "teaching to the test"—has become the orthodox political solution, embraced by both parties. (Senator Edward Kennedy voted for President Bush's NCLB legislation, which the President, in one of the debates, famously described as a "jobs" bill.)

Part and parcel of the push toward privatization is a fundamental redefinition of citizenship and of the parameters of governmental responsibility within American society. For decades, the Republicans and allies in the business community labored mightily to reduce government's role in American life. It is a measure of their success that faith in democratic government has largely been replaced by faith in the market. The Ownership Society became the motto for a dramatic change in the way conservatives viewed government and particularly for their view of the U.S. Department of Education. Jimmy Carter first established the Department of Education as a separate cabinet office, with its own secretary, in 1979. During the 1980 presidential campaign, Ronald Reagan promised to abolish the fledgling Department of Education, dubbing it, "President Carter's new bureaucratic boondoggle."

By the advent of President Bush's first term (2000), conservatives were growing concerned about the burgeoning bloat in the education budget.

> Conservatives need to consider the ominous prospects of expanding federal power over education. Federal funds for character education may sound fine now, but imagine what that might mean under, say, a "Hillary" administration,

warned the Cato Institute's Dan Lips.[37] However, once in power, the new conservatives weren't terribly worried about the prospect of Hillary's administration. They had just been handed a seven-course meal on a silver tray, and they weren't about to throw it out just so the Democrats, should they ever return to power, wouldn't get their hands on it.

Instead, the DOE was transformed into a web of relationships between government and private contractors. Education bureaucrats, like their counterparts at the Pentagon, moved easily between government and corporate offices. A fine example was Assistant Secretary of Education, a former employee of a Pennsylvania loan company and a for-profit education contractor dependent on student loans. According to the *Wall Street Journal*, Sally Stroup received warnings from the Department's Inspector General urging her to curb any "illegal inducements" lenders might be using to win college loan business. Instead, Stroup ignored the advice.[38]

However, there is no better example of Ownership Society abuse of educational standards than in the implementation of "Reading First," the Education Department's reading program. Reading First was launched under Secretary Rod Paige and continued under Paige's successor Margaret Spellings. The billion-dollar-a-year program, like many DOE initiatives, was said to be thoroughly "research-based" and "scientifically tested." Congressional investigators however, exposed a foundation of political cronyism rather than research and effective literacy programs. Reading First has proven to be little more than a channel for lucrative contracts to like-minded private providers of services, using the cudgel of "research-based instruction" to beat back resistance from states and local school districts.

"The No Child Left Behind Act refers to scientifically based programs over 100 times," observed Mark Hayes, a spokesman for a concerned Senator Richard G. Lugar (R-Indiana), one of a bipartisan group of federal lawmakers to request a GAO audit of Reading First.[39]

States received more than $4.8 billion in Reading First grants during the Bush administration, in a tangled process by which some states had to apply for grants as many as six times before receiving approval. DOE officials stacked panels with experts tied to favored publishers. In one e-mail message cited in the report, from which the Inspector General deleted some vulgarities, the director of Reading First, Chris Doherty, urged staff members to make clear to one company that it was not favored at the department:

"They are trying to crash our party and we need to beat the [expletive deleted] out of them in front of all the other would-be party crashers who are standing on the front lawn waiting to see how we welcome these dirtbags," Doherty wrote. He soon was forced to resign from the department to "return to the private sector." Paige's replacement, Margaret Spellings, denied any and all responsibility for "some of the actions taken by department officials" and "individual mistakes." One clip from a Reading First report has Secretary Paige sicking "our barracuda types" on a grant reviewer who was suspected of not going along with the bid rigging.[40]

Congressional investigators found that Reading First contracts were awarded by the administration on the basis of politics and financial ties, not merit. "They designed it for their friends and cronies, and they ended up not designing the best program for America's schoolchildren," said Congressman George Miller (D-California), the chairman of the House Education and Labor Committee, who called the program "a criminal enterprise."

Though reading scores improved slightly in some states, it was revealed that the program evaluators were among those profiting from the program, thus casting doubt over even those modest improvements. Secretary Spellings tried to pass off the

Reading First scandal as an aberration or "mistakes" by a few individuals, but ongoing investigations revealed a pattern of corruption that went far beyond this one program. Conservative think-tankers Chester Finn and Mike Petrilli of the Fordham Foundation had hailed the appointment of Doherty, a former Baltimore operator of a string of charter schools, whom they called a "smart, savvy and a strong advocate for education reform." They continued to defend Doherty and Reading First and justify its manipulation of the grant review panels in the name of enforcing high standards and research-based instruction. Finn had actually set the precedent for this type of official misbehavior during the Reagan administration. In a recent post on his Gadfly blog, Finn boasts:

> When I was an assistant education secretary back in the late medieval period, I spent perhaps a third of my time selecting peer reviewers and panels that had a fighting chance of doing things differently, doing things right—and doing things the way I thought they should be done. Staying out of the legal rough, sure, but absolutely not hitting down the middle of the fairway. That's why I was there.[41]

The Washington watchdog group Citizens for Responsibility and Ethics in Washington criticized the Reading First shenanigans in the strongest terms, bringing suit against the Education Department for the release of documents and, according to its own statements,

> to force the Department of Education to come clean about the extent to which cronyism and corruption have permeated the Reading First panels, potentially depriving our nation's highest risk children of the best possible reading materials.[42]

Melanie Sloan, executive director of the nonprofit organization and a former U.S. Attorney in D.C., charged: "It is becoming increasingly clear that the Bush administration has been sacrificing the education of children to financially benefit a select group of loyalists and donors."[43]

The Reading First scandal was just that—a scandal—because of sloppiness rooted in the extreme arrogance of functionaries, but it was hardly an aberration. The pattern of Ownership Society patronage, abuse of power, and use of politically aligned programs to shape education policy splashed over into after-school tutoring programs, increasingly the domain of a private industry that Senator Hillary Clinton characterized as "Halliburton all over again."[44] Though the comparison between after-school tutoring and Halliburton's war profiteering may seem like a stretch, it's actually not so farfetched. The half-billion a year in tutoring dollars is certainly no match for Halliburton's $24 billion in government contracts, but the operating parallels are striking.

Senator Clinton, who supported the NCLB legislation, pointed out, "Nobody's looking over their shoulder. And we're not really seeing results." Speaking to New Hampshire members of the NEA, she demanded,

> Why would we outsource helping our kids to unaccountable private sector providers? They don't have to follow our civil rights laws, their employees don't even have to be qualified, they aren't required to coordinate with educators, there's a grand total of zero evidence that they're doing any good.

Many of the providers have close ties to the Republican Party and President Bush, she told reporters later.

> It's not enough that there are no-bid contracts that are taking money away from our troops and not delivering services to them in the field, now we have these contracts going to these cronies who are chosen largely on a political basis, and we have nothing to show for it.

The revelations over Reading First and the federal after-school tutoring program were indicative of what the small-schools movement had been experiencing for the previous seven years. It was clear that those of us who held to the community-engagement approach to small schools and who opposed the privately managed version of charter schools were the "dirtbags" and on the outs when it came to major funding initiatives.

The small-schools movement, as part of the larger movement for school reform, always risked getting caught up in this culture. Every school reform organization would ultimately have to choose whether to throw in with the privatizers or risk being isolated and cut off from badly needed resources. We were under pressure from both funders and private industry competitors, who saw the potential for profit and for turning what we had begun into a growth industry. However, in the early days of this reform, we had no idea what lay in store for the gathering movement. The air was charged with optimism, fueled by urgency, and encouraged by early grants to seed the work. Little did we know how the sands would shift. Small schools pioneer Deborah Meier reflected on the looming transformation of small and charter school realities:

> I thought small schools was one reform no one could do harm with...I saw them as representing new ideas and new relationships between the constituents to schooling. I thought of Ted Sizer's little Parker school in Fort Devons, Massachusetts, and a half dozen other little schools I immediately loved. I forgot about the little independent bookstores in my neighborhood that have been replaced by the Barnes and Nobles' of the world. Most charters became the property of those with capital, who reinvented the same old system without a democratic public base.[45]

From the beginning, we were committed to a strategy of systemic change and not just interested in starting one or a few new alternative or charter schools. Our tactics focused on engaging, rather than "blowing up," the existing schools system, along with administrators, teachers, students, and parents, in a movement for educational and social change. We chose to call ourselves a workshop, rather than a program, so as to make it clear that we were not about top-down reforms. A workshop is a learning community that emphasizes problem-solving, hands-on training and requires the involvement of the participants. We hoped this approach would provide a clear alternative to the change strategies and tactics of the top-down reformers.

By 2007, mention of the Ownership Society had all but disappeared from conservative rhetoric. The failure to "reform" Social Security after nearly two full terms of the Bush regime and a majority Republican congress; growing disenchantment with the war in Iraq; and the collapse of the housing market all combined to take the wind out of Ownership Society sails. As new realities set in, including dawning recognition by many that charter schools run by EMOs were not the cure-all they promised to be, new discussions among policy makers and funders began to shift the focus of school reform back to a more balanced perspective. In the months leading up to the 2008 presidential elections, Democrats who had formerly supported and defended the NCLB have come out swinging against its one-sided emphasis on testing and its punitive approach to accountability. New approaches based more on multiple and varied measures of assessment appear to have gained momentum.

At the June 2007 convention of the NEA, the nation's largest teachers union, one Democratic candidate after another lashed out at the existing law. Teachers wearing buttons that read "A child is more than a test score" cheered wildly as Senator Chris Dodd called for a complete overhaul, as candidate John Edwards exclaimed, "These tests do not tell us what we need to know about our children," and as Senator Hillary Rodham Clinton said, "The test is becoming the curriculum when it should be the other way around." Senator Barack Obama closed out the session with a plea for real school reform: "Don't label a school as failing one day and then walk away and throw your hands up the next."

With vouchers no longer a viable alternative to "failing schools," Plan B would be privately managed charter schools to replace hundreds or thousands of closed schools in cities from Washington, D.C. to San Francisco. This would require a takeover of a charter-school movement that began a progressive, teacher-led initiative only a decade earlier.

The role of private management companies supplanting the early teacher-created charter schools, replacing them with top-down replications, is of particular significance to us. In the next chapter, we reveal the way in which the small-schools movement—essentially a movement to create new schools— risks being turned into a school-closing movement in many urban school districts and how its early orientation toward teacher empowerment, educational equity, and social justice is under fire from the Ownership Society.

3

CHARTERING PRIVATE MANAGEMENT

From a December 12, 2006 help-wanted ad on Craig's List from an Oakland, privately managed charter school looking for teachers.

> Multi-cultural specialist, self-esteem experts, liberal progressives or their "klan" relatives need not apply. We want to educate minority students with high academic skills and not brainwash them with nonsense or rhetoric. Do you understand our philosophy?

A new wave of privately managed, rapidly replicated charter schools stands in sharp contrast to the ideas of the early charter- and small-schools visionaries. The foregoing ad reminds us that the small-schools movement remains contested territory. In many districts around the country, the best of the small and charter schools have indeed become agents of change, responding to a national sense that the traditional system of public education needs transformation. Charter schools are supposed to be public schools with a mission—innovate, empower, engage, and succeed in places where traditional schools have not succeeded. They were also intended to spark competition within school systems seemingly inoculated against change by pressuring district administrators to streamline bloated bureaucracie and improve measurable learning outcomes or risk losing students and dollars.

However, the new millennium has seen this promising movement all but replaced by an emerging cottage (and not-so-cottage) industry of for-profit companies, charter school managers (Charter Management Organizations (CMOs)) trying to take ownership of the charter school idea and lay claim to the innovations and creations of public school educators.

Charter schools, which were created as incubators of public school reform, as public teaching-learning laboratories, are now competing with traditional public schools for space, for students, for teachers, principals, and funding. Many have become essentially private schools run on public money, with little or no public accountability. Only a few remain teacher-friendly, with collective bargaining rights for teachers and participation from engaged communities.

Our purpose in this chapter, however, is not to lambaste small schools or charter schools as a group. We remain small-schools advocates and practitioners, aware of the need for systemic change, and hopeful about the prospects of the former though obviously less so about those of the latter. Advocates and practitioners, however, are not the same as cheerleaders. We want these new schools to be good schools and not clones of systemic inequality.

As we will explain, we don't believe there is much validity in evaluating entire groups of schools solely on the basis of their charter or non-charter status, any more than it is valid to compare American schools to those in Slovenia. Though such often sensational comparisons are the rage among business-model reformers and in the mass media, they usually ignore the reality that there are two tiers of public education in this country and that public schools aren't all one thing. They also ignore the realities of life outside of school and place the weight of academic success purely on the school itself. Our top-tier schools, usually found in upscale, higher-income communities, spend two or three times what inner-city or rural schools spend on each child's education and can compete with any schools in the world. Neighborhood public schools, with skilled teachers, reasonable size, and adequate resources easily outperform charter schools without those ingredients.

A *New York Times* story about Briarcliff Middle School, a small public school in upscale Westchester County, illustrates our point. The story, part of a *New York Times* series called "The Critical Years," was all about the challenges of middle-school education. Briarcliff was heralded as "a nationally recognized model of a middle school that gets things right." The article described the wealth of programs and resources available to Briarcliff's kids and the school's focus on a "habits of the mind" curriculum. It then pointed out:

> Briarcliff school starts out with many advantages. It is part of a district in Westchester County that spends $24,738 per student, or more than one and a half times the New York State average, and can afford to buy extra sets of classroom textbooks so that students can leave their own copies at home. Its student body is relatively homogenous—91.8 percent are white—and so well off that less than 1 percent qualify for free or reduced lunches. In contrast, in nearby New York City, 72 percent of the population qualifies.[1]

Briarcliff is obviously a good school, but it is also a school that chooses, directly or indirectly, its students, if by no other standard, than by the zip code of their parent's house. Briarcliff's kids could probably compete with kids in Finland or Japan when it comes to math and reading scores. Schools such as Briarcliff don't have to go charter to accomplish their mission. It's a school that clearly reflects the values of its community and has the support from families who can afford to live in that community. That's why you will rarely see charter schools in wealthy school districts.

Often drowned out or downplayed amid the hype about charter school superiority over neighborhood public schools, coming mainly from the No Child crowd and from charter school associations, is the strong, emerging body of research available on charter schools, largely based on comparative standardized test scores, with results not measurably better than those in the traditional schools they were meant to replace, and often worse. In particular, those managed by the CMOs have failed to produce any significant measurable improvements and often at a significantly higher costs, financially and socially.

In Connecticut, for example, the percentage of charter students meeting targets on early (1997–2002) Connecticut Mastery Tests and Connecticut Academic Performance Test were well below the state average. Though it could be argued that these studies are dated and that it takes time for improvements to work, the point is only that they belie the claims that charters are inherently, or as a group, superior to the neighborhood schools they replaced. If they were just seen as experiments, their mitigating effects on other public schools would be taken into account. When students choose to go to state charter schools, their towns may suffer the loss of state education cost-sharing grants for those students. At the same time, the students' hometown school districts are responsible for the students' transportation to the charter schools and also some special education costs at the state schools. So there is a net loss to these children's hometown school budgets—a shortfall that local taxpayers have to make up.

Other early studies, like the one based on data from 2003 on students' performance on the National Assessment of Educational Progress, found many charter school students significantly behind their non-charter school counterparts. It also showed that, on average, charter schools that were affiliated with public school districts performed just as well as did traditional public schools.

Charter school advocates may again argue that test scores aren't the best way to measure school success, a point well taken, though an argument usually mocked by those same advocates when used to evaluate traditional public schools operating in poor neighborhoods. Their argument not only demonstrates the folly of using standardized test scores as the single measure of school success but shows that many of the charter school associations have developed a narrow group interest of their own, weakening our early hopes for a community of interests with the rest of public education. Charter advocates can't responsibly use test-score results to batter neighborhood public schools and then discredit their use to compare them with charters.

It could also be said that if public school bureaucracies had the will and the capacity to reform themselves, charter schools would become irrelevant. As we shall show, it's fruitless for educators and communities to oppose charter schools willy-nilly or even to stand against privatization without offering a public school reform strategy of their own. Any such strategy, as we elaborate in Chapter 6, will have to accept charter schools as a critical force in school reform while relying on active community engagement to keep them public. In a small but growing number of large urban districts such as Boston, New York, and Los Angeles, district leaders, parent groups, and teacher unions have formed alliances with more progressive, non-profit CMOs as a way of heading off the privatizers.

A large number of school superintendents, now often called CEOs, have however opened the door and the district budget to privatizers and the CMOs as a way of taking the onus off themselves for perceived school failure. One big-city superintendent recently told us that Chicago small schools would be better off as managed private companies so they could "free themselves from our bureaucratic interference." There was no need to ask him, "Why don't you just stop interfering?" We knew the honest answer would be, "We can't help ourselves."

Conversely, public schools are too valuable an asset in a democratic society to be handed over en mass to private operators, many of whom have no track record of success and may be doing great harm. In the final analysis, it will be an engaged school community that determines the future of this public education reform.

In this chapter, we show how the small-schools movement now faces the loss of its early democratic vision as it increasingly looks to the forces of privatization, the No Child Left Behind (NCLB), and venture philanthropy for rescue. Moves to close hundreds of urban schools in cities such as Detroit, Chicago, Los Angeles, and New York have come almost exclusively in poor black and Hispanic neighborhoods and mainly are done for cost savings rather than often-stated academic reasons. The closings coincide with plans for neighborhood gentrification and offers by redevelopment forces to build chains of new charter schools in the same neighborhood. In Detroit, the plan is to shutter fifty buildings in predominantly African-American neighborhoods, often taking away not just a school but an essential community resource from an already depleted community. In their place, ed-entrepreneurs such as billionaire philanthropist Bob Thompson propose investing $200 million in the creation of fifteen new charter schools. Without a reform plan of its own, a cash-starved Detroit Public Schools (DPS) and the local teachers union don't have solid ground to stand on in their opposition to the plan. Their only hope lies in the strength of community resistance.

Many of the new small schools have become "big schools in drag," according to CUNY professor, researcher, and small-schools activist Michelle Fine. She reminds us that "the small schools movement was never simply about size."[2] After surveying the current field of small and charter schools, she finds that:

> all too many small schools have the same authoritarian principals, disempowered and uninspired educators, dubious high-stakes tests, and Eurocentric curricula as the large schools they were designed to replace.

To make matters even worse, these big schools in drag are actually bigger in reality. Though the charter-school movement was built on the notion that smaller is better, recent studies suggests that for-profit charters, the fastest growing segment of the market, are replicating some aspects of both the size of public schools and the centralized top-down decision making of the public school system.

A 2005 study in the *Social Sciences Quarterly* study, based on a survey of all charters in the states of Arizona, Michigan, and Pennsylvania and in Washington, D.C., found that charters started by for-profit education management organizations (EMOs), were indeed different from other charter schools in several important and fundamental ways. EMO-founded charter schools, for example, were more than 80 percent larger than others, most of which were more "mission-oriented" schools (those founded by a social service agency or a community of like-minded teachers and parents who are devoted to a common purpose, such as teaching methodology or racial or ethnic identity).[3]

According to the report, in for-profit charters, decisions about facilities, curriculum, testing, and student discipline were less likely to be made at the school level. According to lead author Jeffrey Henig:

> Charter schools are an interesting and potentially important policy experiment, incorporating a diverse array of sub-experiments, some of which may be very worthy of emulation...But...it is also true...that some charter schools are failing on multiple dimensions, that some careful studies find no positive impact on test scores or positive competitive effect on traditional school systems, and that there is a lot about the phenomenon that we simply do not yet understand.

Though EMO-run charter schools currently make up about one-fourth of all charters, in some states they already dominate the field. In Michigan, for example, the EMOs run about 75 percent of the state's 230 or so charter schools. The number is so high owing in part to the number of state universities willing and able to become chartering agencies, despite wide-scale teacher opposition and protest. A proposal to create fifteen new charter schools in Detroit in 2003 drew protests from more than 3,000 public school teachers who missed work to attend a rally at the state capital. However, despite this vocal opposition, parent demand remains a strong factor in driving political support for charter school growth.

The locomotive driving the for-profit charter train has been Edison Schools, Inc. Edison Schools were started in 1992 by entrepreneur founder Chris Whittle. Whittle, often called the guru of captive-audience marketing because of his advertising strategies in doctors' offices and shopping malls, originally had planned to open 1,000 small private schools that would compete with public schools by offering government vouchers to enable poor students to avoid the heavy tuition costs. However, as vouchers were dropped as a significant part of the administration's reform plan, Whittle and partner Beno Schmidt dropped the private school plan in favor of turning Edison into an EMO for charter schools.

Despite a spotty track record, one that exemplifies the Henig study, Edison continues to receive huge contracts to operate urban charter schools. One of its early failures—a real debacle—was its Boston Renaissance Charter School, a middle-school with more than 1,000 students and run by Edison until the district severed its contract in 2002, three years before it was supposed to expire. Eighth-graders at Renaissance performed below state and district averages—69 percent failed the statewide math test, compared with 54 percent in the Boston school district and 31 percent in the state; in English, 22 percent of Renaissance eighth-graders failed, compared with 20 percent citywide and 8 percent statewide. However, beyond poor measurable learning outcomes, Renaissance also engaged in practices that could be called barbaric, practices well documented by researcher Peggy Farber in a series of Kappan articles:

> The practices included bridling disruptive kindergartners in restraining holds; interrupting classes with a school-wide alarm called Code Orange whenever a teacher sensed control slipping; suspending students at all grade levels, including kindergarten and first grade, assigning students—by the dozen—to an all-day detention room for months at a time; and bullying parents who objected to such practices.[4]

Michelle Fine points to a "new phase" in the small-schools movement that runs counter to its bottom-up origins, a phase that is top-down and privately subsidized. Fine says:

> It's branded as "systemic reform" but doesn't reform the system. There is an industry afoot to mass produce and export "small" across urban zip codes, without much thinking about how to create a just system of quality schools for urban youth.[5]

A *New York Times* editorial, "Exploding the Charter School Myth," raised the specter of free-standing charter schools biting off more than they can chew:

> The presumption is that without the bureaucratic restraints of the public school system and the teacher unions, charter schools can provide better education at lower cost. But the problem with failing public schools is that they often lack both resources and skilled, experienced teachers. While there are obvious exceptions, some charter schools embark on a path that simply recreates the failures of the schools they were developed to replace.[6]

New York Times writer Samuel Freedman reports that small and charter schools, under Mayor Bloomberg's reform plan, have systematically excluded immigrants and English-language learners (ELLs).[7] The Mayor's plan has led to the closing of schools with large immigrant populations, gutting their ELL programs and packing them off to other large, under-resourced schools that cannot offer the kind of instruction to which they are entitled. Recent studies show a similar negative impact on special education students and those with disabilities.[8]

Many other early pioneers and small-schools advocates have grown disenchanted or uneasy with what they see as a new phase of mass reproduction and privatization of small schools, a phase, we would argue, directly tied to the onset of the Ownership Society.

The charter school movement, which began as an experiment in teacher empowerment and parental choice nearly twenty years ago, has, like all areas of school reform, became a political minefield. The reason? There's so much at stake, educationally, financially, and politically.

Charter schools began as part of a progressive movement of educators trying to escape the tyranny of the large school bureaucracies and provide new and better options for parents and students. In a recent interview, school pioneer Joe Nathan told us, "We wanted to empower families in poor, urban communities, to create options—the kind that more affluent suburban families have always had."[9]

The original charters were largely an outgrowth of the small-school movement and, at one time, were practically synonymous with small schools. Like small schools or learning communities, charters were originally imagined as incubators of change and innovation by an unusual collection of education activists who crossed the political spectrum, such as Fine, Nathan, Albert Shanker, Ted Kolderie, and Ray Budde, to name but a few.

Most saw themselves as progressives and proponents of educational equity and excellence. Their fundamentally democratic idea was to create an open sector of small public schools that might provide parents and students with choices and teachers with more control of their learning environment. It would serve to encourage them to use innovative teaching techniques and practices geared more toward the learning styles of individual students and to take direct responsibility for those students' academic success. The open-sector idea came from Kolderie, who saw the complete autonomy of these new schools and a consumer model of choice as the keys to their success. "But choice," said Nathan, "is a powerful tool that must be handled carefully. Remember, it was choice that created private academies in the south in support of school segregation."

Many of us viewed the original charters as a critical force within public education, a force for sharing ideas and resources with more traditional public schools and serving as centers for teachers' professional development. We also felt that if a small group of charter schools could push the envelope on things such as mandated testing while successfully educating students from low-income families, they could open new avenues for systemic reform. In our scheme of things, the early charters were an important part of a larger, small-schools strategy that might soften the hold the bureaucracy and teachers union had on the change process by getting unnecessary work rules changed or eliminated (through a teacher vote), reducing the size of the union contract, and allowing for more flexibility on staffing.

However, progressives weren't the only ones dreaming about charters. Other more conservative forces, claiming to be the new education "radicals," also envisioned charters as a way to "blow up the system." Some saw charter schools as a new and more subtle way to sort and track kids or as a doorway to school vouchers, privatization of public systems, and as an end to unions altogether. They also imagined them as a new and growing marketplace wherein for-profit educational management companies could compete with traditional models of bureaucratic management.

Profits with little or few risks or start-up costs—the equivalent of buying failed companies on the cheap, dismantling them or running them more efficiently at a profit, leveraging loans against school real estate, selling special education services, after-school programs, textbooks, and testing services —what more could such new education entrepreneurs as Edison's Chris Whittle ask for in the new business environment?

With hopes fading for the passage of a national school voucher program, one that might have supported a chain of 1,000 private Edison schools, anti-"government school" forces saw charters as their fall-back position. Whittle was far afield of the libertarian and traditional right-wingers who simply wanted alternatives to "government schools" or aimed at curtailing what they perceived as the growing federal power over public education and states rights.

Whittle, along with a host of other for-profit school operators, saw a necessarily stronger role for the federal government in education, a stronger, more influential role than it had at any previous point in history. In his book, *Crash Course* (2005),[10] Whittle calls on the federal government to become much more involved in developing new school designs that local districts might choose to adopt. With some of the largest Wall Street investors behind them, plenty of powerful political friends at the federal and state levels, and big promises of computers and classroom discipline in all his new schools, Whittle and Edison seemed to be on solid ground in expecting these local districts to opt for them. They hoped that the chaotic "choice" and transfer provisions of the NCLB Law would also feed them thousands of new students.

Early charter and small-school advocates had no way of anticipating this kind of rough-and-tumble politics with multi-million-dollar stakes or of knowing how the battlefield would shift when the neo-cons of the Bush administration took over the U.S. Department of Education in 2000. The early charter schoolers, mainly teachers and parents, were certainly not prepared to enter the world of high-stakes, expand-or-die charter replication. That would of necessity be left to the CMOs.

New charter schools were at first accountable only to their local school districts. Later, charter leaders such as Nathan and Kolderie would be successful in many states in pushing for multiple charter authorizers to be included in state charter laws. Nominal systems, varying from state to state, were put in place, with the aim of making charters more accountable. If a school failed to produce or live up to its own mission, it could be subject to remediation efforts, have its charter revoked, or be closed down. As districts, especially suburban districts, grew resistant to what they perceived as a threat to their own funding and control and as caps were enacted to constrain charter school growth, the CMOs negotiated their right to group dozens of schools under one charter. Chains of charter schools made it almost impossible to hold schools accountable as scores became averaged across the chain and reporting systems broke down.

With the 2002 NCLB Law, charter elementary schools were supposed to be held to many of the same accountability measurements as other schools. Where that occurred, charters as a group fared no better than do other public schools.

In a 1996 book, Nathan wrote,

> Hundreds of charter schools have been created around this nation by educators who are willing to put their jobs on the line, to say, 'If we can't improve students' achievement, close down our school.' That is accountability — clear, specific, and real.[11]

Had the progressives really bought into Milton Friedman's dream of market-driven schooling wherein schools would no longer depend on the state for quality control and where public resources and institutions would be forced out of business by market pressures? We've never seen Nathan's survey, wherein teachers expressed their willingness to join the unemployment line if their kids' test scores were low, so we can't dispute his claim. However, though there may have been little thought given to what effects any such closures might have on local communities or on the reform movement itself, this trade-off— autonomy for accountability—was the heart of early charter school governance plans.

Ray Budde, a University of Massachusetts education professor who died in 2005, is credited with coining the term *charter schools*. Budde never dreamed that charters could ever offer a real alternative to the public education system. He hoped instead, like Shanker, Nathan, and Fine, that the charter arrangement might result in a new type of school and, in some cases, produce alternative district structure that would give schools more autonomy and teachers increased responsibility over curriculum and instruction in exchange for a greater degree of accountability for student achievement.[12]

Ray Budde's proposal called for a restructuring of the school district, for shrinking the levels of command down to two levels in which groups of teachers would receive educational charters directly from local school boards and would take responsibility for instruction. Budde's plan wasn't about union busting or pulling schools, teachers, and students out of existing schools. It was a concept akin to the latter-day pilot schools in cities such as Boston and Los Angeles, an inside–outside partnership and one that the Education Commission of the States would refer to as the "all-charter district."

Minnesota became the first state to create new charter schools with leadership coming from Kolderie and Nathan, who were based at the University of Minnesota, and to receive bipartisan support in the state legislature. In 1991, Minnesota's U.S. Senator Dave Durenberger, a Republican, brought the charter idea to Washington, joining forces with Connecticut's Democratic U.S. Senator Joseph Lieberman to introduce what became the federal charter school grant program. That legislation, adopted in 1994 with strong support from the Clinton administration, added further encouragement to states to pass and implement charter laws. In a 1995 tribute to Budde, Kolderie wrote:

> As the new-schools idea spread, people asked Ray Budde how he felt about what had happened with his idea. For some years he would say: "This is not what I originally had in mind." But by the time of his 1996 Kappan article his feelings had changed. "There are more powerful dynamics at work in creating a whole new school than in simply restructuring a department or starting a new program," he wrote. He saw that the states were creating an expanding movement "challenging the traditional form of organization of the local school district." Which of course was what he originally had in mind. Ray Budde continued to hope the decentralized model would come to be used by districts, too; felt this was important to revitalizing district public education. Call it chartering or site-management, there is "a necessity of placing more decision-making at the school level, close to the classrooms."[13]

Kolderie, the leader of the early charter school movement in Minnesota, was at first cautiously optimistic about the prospects for charters. However, after the Clintons sent their daughter, Chelsea, to private school rather than to any D.C. public school, Kolderie sent a commentary to the *Washington Post*, which they never published.[14] The commentary, which used many of the same arguments that school voucher advocates had used a decade earlier, pointed out how the rich and powerful already had lots of options denied to poor people. He offered charter schools as a real democratic alternative to the district's horrible public schools, schools that he thought could never be reformed or fixed from within, through neither organizational changes nor leadership changes. The *Post*'s rejection of his letter confirmed for Kolderie that charter school advocates were a lone voice in the wilderness that might never be heard. It was this sense of isolation and a circle-the-wagons mentality, along with early problems of school management, that would later help to push a significant sector of charter-school movement into the arms of the CMOs.

Ironically, it was Clinton and the Democrats who would soon jump on the charter school bandwagon, with Clinton calling for a tripling of the number of charters schools by the year 2010. His estimate proved to be conservative. Charters would grow from what neo-con think-tanker and former Assistant Secretary of Education Chester "Checker" Finn would describe as a movement of early "plucky charter founders" trying to "overcome adversity"[15] into a mélange of competing, professional school management companies. A decade later, this cottage industry would begin to shake out. Larger companies, operating with huge grants from private foundations and solid political support from the President of the United States down through federal and state agencies would gradually take over the playing field.

The strongest opposition would come from local boards of education who felt threatened by competition for students (especially under NCLB provisions that encouraged students to leave their home school if it failed to make annual yearly progress) and the tax dollars that followed them. Another strong base for opposition were the teachers unions, most of whose leaders didn't share Al Shanker's charter vision.

Unlike Kolderie, who wanted the legislature to pass charter laws to force school districts into ceding authority over the new schools, American Federation of Teachers President Shanker, a fairly traditional educator and national standards advocate, viewed charters as experimental models, still closely affiliated with school districts. Though many conservatives saw charters as a stepping stone toward vouchers, Shanker saw them as a way to stave off vouchers.

According to Nathan, who had worked with Shanker in New York, the union was strongly influenced by Ray Budde's ideas on empowering teachers to create innovative new programs.[16] Shanker and other far-sighted union leaders thought charters had great potential as a strategy for school improvement, one that would bring together the union, the school board, and the parents to fix local schools. He proposed that teachers start new schools in existing school buildings. However, as Nathan pointed out, Shanker was also aware of the pressures teachers would face when and if they moved toward new innovative small schools.

Early charter experiments began in Philadelphia's high schools in 1988. That year, fewer than half of Philadelphia's ninth graders even made it to the tenth grade. In many schools, more than a fourth of incoming ninth graders were sixteen years old or older, and nearly a third had been tagged as needing special education.

The Philadelphia Schools Collaborative pushed Super-intendent Connie Clayton to create its version of charter schools inside many of the city's large, struggling high schools, using willing teachers and students to drive the reform forward. However, these early charters were a far cry from those we see today. Philly's early charters were synonymous with highly autonomous small schools or schools-within-a-school, created and run by teachers, not management companies. They were created without legislation or top-down mandates. Collaborative leader Michelle Fine wrote:

> Our task was to reinvigorate intellectually and professionally the educators who had survived typically 20 years in these anonymous and disempowering institutions, to reengage the students "left behind" who attended (and did not attend) these schools, and to organize the parents who were attached to (and alienated from) the institutions of deep dispair and not infrequent hostility.[17]

Ironically, this early attempt at Shanker-style charter school creation was met with suspicion and hostility from the leadership of Philadelphia's teachers union, especially after Clayton retired and David Hornbeck, an aggressive reformer, took over the reins as superintendent. Conservative Governor Tom Ridge, who would later lead a state takeover of Philadelphia's public schools, pushed for a freeze on school funding, making any kind of reform all the more difficult. As Fine and other members of the Collaborative (and all of us) would later find out, it's very difficult to talk about reform when teaching positions are being cut, schools are being closed, and hundreds of teachers are losing their jobs.

With Hornbeck pushing back and mandating reform from the top of the system, the charter movement, as a grassroots, teacher-led reform initiative, hit the wall. The Collaborative, which had received heavy funding from the Pew Charitable Trust, collapsed. A decade later, it would be neo-con Governor Ridge himself who would be pushing the new model of privately managed charters led by Edison Schools, Inc. on a first resistant and later an acquiescent superintendent, Paul Vallas and on a compliant group of the same Philadelphia Federation of Teachers (PFT) union leaders. Philadelphia would become a harbinger of things to come for the small-schools movement nationally.

By 2007, there were 4,000 charter schools in forty states and the District of Columbia, with heavy concentrations in the most politically conservative areas of states such as Texas, Arizona, and Ohio. California had the most charter schools (575) but faced a crisis when more than 100, including its largest, were shut down for financial mismanagement.

Faced with growing opposition from teachers unions and local school boards, as well as big problems in securing facilities, funding, and staff, charter school leaders increasingly began to see themselves as a group under assault from the system, with common interests quite apart from regular public schools. Local and national charter school associations formed with their own funding streams that included healthy federal and private grants and growing political support from both political parties and the business sector.

Charter school associations grew, armed with a sense of purpose and a common interest quite apart from their parent public school districts. Full disclosure and transparency soon would be translated as advertising and putting one's best face on in public. Communications experts and firms began to show up on the roster of nearly all charter schools, associations, and chartering agencies. Their job—compare charters to neighborhood public schools, making as strong a case as possible for the superiority of charters as a class. The war between "public" and "charters" was on, in charter brochures, flyers, and editorials in the local and national media.

This loss of charter-school accountability was well documented by early charter advocates and critics alike, but for different reasons. Finn and his colleagues at the Fordham Foundation wrote in 1996 that they had "yet to see a single state with a thoughtful and well-formed plan for evaluating its charter school program."[18] Finn, who directed the conservative Fordham Foundation (which, ignoring conflicts of interest, would later emerge as a major charter school operator in its own right), observed four years later, "Charter school discussions are saturated with talk about accountability. Some view it as the third rail of the charter movement, some as the holy grail."[19] Finn put the responsibility for this failure not on the political and economic necessities of the charters but on public school systems themselves, proving once again to his ardent followers that reform, outside of privatization, wasn't really possible.

Gerald Bracy described the Finn group approach this way:

> They proposed something they call "accountability by transparency," whereby "the school routinely and systematically discloses complete, accurate, and timely information about its program, performance, and organization." Their system, though, requires so much information in the form of various test scores, progress toward goals, student standards, curriculum, instructional methods, demographic characteristics, and more that it would seem to eviscerate the original concept of a charter school.[20]

Ironically, it was Finn's Fordham Foundation that blasted the Clinton administration when it investigated Edison's Renaissance Charter School in Boston in 1997. The DOE found violations of special-education students' civil rights and patterns of racial discrimination in the school. However, Fordham rose to Edison's defense and blasted Clinton's Office of Civil Rights for their "witch hunt" against Renaissance. So much for "accountability." The Boston school district followed up the investigation by severing its ties with Edison.

In a speech to Louisiana's post-Katrina state school board, a more level-headed Greg Richmond, president of the National Association of Charter School Authorizers, pushed for a more balanced view of charters:

> Some of the success that networks of charters have shown in motivating minority and low-income learners is astounding and reflects entrepreneurial education at its finest. But there has been enough failure and excess in some charter settings that a degree of humility is called for as well. Are we maturing enough to face ourselves and admit our mistakes? Is it time to tone down the in-your-face challenges to the status quo? Might we study the results and civilly and honestly explain what we have learned? If we do, might districts begin to use chartering strategically to move entire public school systems forward?[21]

Today, it appears that most of the CMOs remain largely unmoved by Richmond's view of the strategic connection between charters and public school improvement or by his calls for humility.

As far back as the 2000 presidential campaign, both candidates Bush and Gore were voicing support for charter schools. However, despite repeated denials, Bush's agenda was clearly geared more toward the privately managed type. The first of the private EMOs was Education Alternatives Inc. (EAI), which attracted national attention when it won ill-fated contracts to manage the Baltimore and Hartford school systems in the early 1990s. The company went public and later collapsed when both contracts were cancelled. EAI had cut the actual teaching staff of schools it had taken over by 20 percent but failed in its objective of raising measurable student achievement.[22]

The next wave of private managers learned some lessons from EAI—simply taking over the central office of existing school districts and ousting superintendents in favor of private-sector managers were not enough to effect decisive improvement. Edison Schools, the first of the second wave of managers, focused on implementing a comprehensive "school design" at each client school and began modestly, opening just four schools in 1992. Most organizations focused on opening only de novo charter schools, built from the ground up. However, like EAI, other EMOs continued to over-promise and under-deliver. They were thwarted by contractual arrangements that, while superior to EAI's, fell far short of providing them the authority they needed to implement their models exactingly. And political resistance from the education establishment remained fierce.[23]

A reporter once asked George W. Bush whether he supported the privatization of public education. The reporter referred specifically to the rapid growth of charter schools operated by for-profit educational management companies in Bush's home state of Texas, which were competing for dollars, students, principals, and teachers with neighborhood public schools. Bush wouldn't answer the question directly but implied that Texas wasn't privatizing education. "In my state," he said, "charter schools are public schools."

Indeed, they were public schools, in the sense that they were supported with public funds. However, what about public responsibility or accountability? Where was the real "public" in those public schools? Also, if they were really public, why were political leaders being continually forced into a line of denial about their public nature?

This line of denial has been used time and time again by local adherents to privatization, such as New York's Mayor Bloomberg. Bloomberg's appointed chancellor, Joel Klein, spearheaded the drive toward private management of public schools. However, even after appointing Edison executive Chris Cerf as his deputy chancellor, when confronted directly with growing parent and community opposition, Klein denied everything. "We're not looking to bring for-profits into the city," Klein told a group of angry parents.[24]

For-profit school management mogul and captive-audience marketing guru Chris Whittle is also a privatization denier who decries the "privatization bogeyman"[25] and hides behind the mysteriously low profit margins that show up on his company's tax returns. Of course, he never mentions the profitablity of his subsidiary companies, such as Channel One, which feed into his Edison Schools.

Michael Scherer, writing for *Mother Jones*, was quick to point out that:

> [M]any charter schools in Texas, while still a part of the public education system, are run by for-profit companies. And many of the biggest shareholders of those firms invested heavily in Bush, who pledged to provide $3 billion in federal loans for new charter schools and to offer subsidies for students to attend private schools. Just as brokers stand to benefit from privatizing Social Security, some of Bush's largest donors would profit from turning education over to the marketplace.[26]

Kent Fischer at the *St. Petersburg Times* wrote:

> The profit motive drives business...More and more, it's driving Florida school reform. The vehicle: charter schools. This was not the plan. These schools were to be "incubators of innovation," free of the rules that govern traditional districts. Local school boards would decide who gets the charters, which spell out how a school will operate and what it will teach. To keep to this ideal, lawmakers specified that only nonprofit groups could get charters. But six years later, profit has become pivotal.
>
> —For-profit corporations create nonprofit foundations to obtain the charters, then hire themselves to run the schools.

—Innovation is no longer the focus. The big companies offer standard curriculums. Critics call their schools "McCharters."

—Developers team with the charter companies to offer home buyers an upscale amenity—tuition-free, taxpayer-funded schools for their developments.

Quietly, lost in the shadow of headline-grabbing vouchers, charter schools have become a hit.[27]

Bush's 2000 campaign had benefited from the early EMOs. Backers of Edison Schools, the largest of the EMOs, contributed heavily to the Republicans. They included John Childs, a Boston financier, who gave $670,000, and Donald Fisher, chairman of the Gap, who gave $260,800, all but $62,800 to the GOP.

Investors in Advantage Schools, one of Edison's chief competitors, also backed the GOP. John Hennessy, whose Credit Suisse First Boston has pumped $19 million into Advantage, took a lead fund-raising role for Bush and contributed $164,000 of his own money to the Republicans. John Doerr gave $477,500, and Kevin Compton of the Silicon Valley venture firm Kleiner, Perkins, Caufield & Byers, which has invested in Advantage, also ventured into politics. Compton gave $143,000 to Republicans, while Doerr supported Gore, who promoted a charter school plan of his own.

"In addition," writes Scherer, "the GOP received large contributions from several of the nation's leading advocates for school vouchers, which provide public funds to students attending private schools."

Richard DeVos, the founder of Amway, put up $10 million of his own money for a failed voucher initiative in Michigan. He also gave $764,500 to Republican campaigns. David Brennan, an industrialist who helped to launch a voucher plan declared unconstitutional by the Ohio Supreme Court and who opened a for-profit charter school company called White Hat Management, contributed $155,500.

Wal-Mart heir John Walton spent millions promoting voucher initiatives, and buyout specialist Theodore Forstmann, who shares ownership of a higher-education for-profit called Capella Education, financed an advertising campaign to promote privatization. The Walton Foundation has since become the largest backer of charters and the single largest source of funding for educational ownership society. Walton funding allows some charter schools to spend more per pupil than "competing" public schools and plays a major role in expanding the two-tiered educational system.

Liza Featherstone, writing in *The Nation*,[28] reveals the mega-company's foundation support for far-right political causes, including its support for EMO schools such as the Knowledge Is Power Program (KIPP) schools. Featherstone singles out the KIPP as an example of Walton's support for "the most mind-numbing and cultish" charter schools. Walton in 2003 gave nearly $3 million to KIPP schools and millions more to other schools using the KIPP curriculum, which according to Featherstone "emphasizes regimented recitation rather than critical or creative thinking."

The piece continues:

> Particularly widespread in low-income neighborhoods, such schools seem bent on disciplining and exhorting the poor rather than developing human potential (much like Wal-Mart as a workplace, with its relentless company cheers and dead-end jobs). Several years ago the principal of New York City's John A. Reisenbach Charter School, which uses the KIPP curriculum and received $118,000 from the Waltons in 2003, told me proudly, as we watched fidgety second graders chant meaningless slogans, "We are getting them ready for business."

Though the KIPP became President Bush's favorite EMO, deserving of a spot on the dais at the Republican national convention, many liberals and progressive educators also touted KIPP schools for their non-profit status and their apparent curricular flexibility. Education writers such as Jay Mathews, by his own admission, swoon whenever KIPP's name is mentioned. Writes Mathews:

> Some critics decry the way the Knowledge Is Power Program presents itself as the savior of inner city education. My answer: KIPP doesn't do that. We sloppy journalists do. Let me present Exhibit A: The latest annual report card from the KIPP Foundation in San Francisco. It has 93 pages of remarkable data. (See, there I go again, making KIPP the miracle cure. Let me change that to "interesting" data.) The report card tells how well each of the KIPP schools is doing, but it does not claim to be saving our cities.[29]

However, once the gloss wears off and the KIPP has to replicate success in more than seventy of it schools and demonstrate that success the same way in which thousands of other regular pubic schools have to, you can find many of the same problems that you find in most neighborhood schools and many others that wouldn't be allowed in regular public schools. The main difference being that if a KIPP school is pulling down test scores or not pulling in enough kids, KIPP can dump them from its rolls. Some might see this as an advantage for the EMO schools. After all, if a branch of Walgreen's or K–Mart wasn't making enough money, you wouldn't think it could last long in today's ownership environment.

Mathews points to KIPP as one of the few EMOs that has a high level of transparency. True enough. However, when Mathews looked at KIPP's report card, here's what he found:

> On page 57 you will find numbers that help explain why KIPP is firing its middle school in Buffalo, N.Y., the sixth time a KIPP school has left the network. The KIPP people put this more gently. In an April 20 letter to

the New York Charter School Association, KIPP chief executive officer Richard Barth said the KIPP Foundation "will end its partnership" with the KIPP Sankofa Charter School in Buffalo "and remove 'KIPP' from the school's name." KIPP spokesman Steve Mancini wished the school well in its plans to continue without the KIPP label. "It is not meeting KIPP standards," he said, "but we think it is providing a viable option for that community."

KIPP was operating a school in decrepit and unsafe facilities in Oakland. Its students were being psychologically abused by KIPP's behavior modification techniques, especially when they were carried out by ill-equipped or novice teachers. African-American boys were leaving KIPP schools at an alarming rate. KIPP was closing seven of its schools because of declining attendance, low performance, or their own staffing and leadership inadequacies. A September 13, 2006 report in the *Rocky Mountain News* detailed the closing of the KIPP-run Cole College Prep Charter in Denver: "By the middle of that school year, December 2005, the school was on its third principal and had lost three of six teachers. Its governing board also had dissolved," wrote *News* reporter Nancy Mitchell.

The *Denver Post* described the school closure this way:

KIPP won the contract to take over Cole Middle School in late 2004 after Cole was shut down by the state for chronic poor performance on state tests. At the time, charter school officials promised to take care of the existing Cole kids. They also promised to open a premier program in the neighborhood in the fall of 2007. The program would have started with fifth-graders. But because the leadership of KIPP—Knowledge Is Power Program—couldn't find a strong principal for northeast Denver, officials decided to shut the school down at the end of spring.[30]

It could be said that the lack of local available leadership was a valid reason to close a school. However, the question of the training and preparation of principals and teacher leaders should be a central part of any charter replication plan. Why didn't KIPP, with its goal of opening dozens, if not hundreds of charter schools nationwide and with seemingly unlimited resources at their disposal, anticipate a leadership shortage and prepare for it? Why should parents and students in one of Denver's neediest communities have to lose a neighborhood public school and bear the burden of KIPP's inefficiency or lack of capacity? Shouldn't that be looked into by charter authorizers before it becomes and community crisis? These are some of the questions that have arisen nationally with the rise of the EMOs and their unchecked replicability initiatives. They have arisen in Chicago with the Renaissance 2010 plan to open 100 new (mainly charter) schools. "Where are the 100 new school leaders going to come from," we asked? Especially in light of district-wide principal retirements and predictable shortages. So far, no response.

Some might argue that KIPP is a not-for-profit corporation as opposed to companies such as Edison, which are openly traded on the stock exchange. However, when it comes to charter school management, there is often a fine line between the two, as well as symbiosis between privateers and non-profits. For example, once they got their charter application approved, the non-profit New Orleans Charter School Foundation immediately went out and hired the Leona Group, a for-profit company with offices in Phoenix, Arizona and East Lansing, Michigan to operate their K–8 school and a high school.

The Leona Group had been hired by a Florida non-profit, the Athenian Academy, to open two charter schools in Pasco County. The company had been fired from its previous charter operations in a Michigan district after test scores plummeted, couldn't get it together in time for a 2005 opening, and had to push the schedule back a year.

However, by hiding behind their partner non-profit, Leona suffered no consequences even though an on-time opening was desperately needed by Katrina-ravaged residents. Despite a spotty record of school management, Leona continues to thrive in the ownership society business climate. According to the *Muskegon Chronicle*,[31]

> Tri-Valley Academy, the county's oldest charter school, used Lansing-based management firm Leona Group for most of its 10-year existence. Last spring, the school board fired Leona, and is expected to submit a new school improvement plan...that reflects the leadership of its new management company.

Since 2005, New Orleans has become a sort of Mecca for the for-profit CMOs operating behind non-profit cover. The Treme Charter School Association, a non-profit, was chartered to open three schools serving children in grades K–5. However, EdFutures, Inc., a San Diego-based for-profit company that runs schools in Atlanta and Delray Beach, Florida, was hired to provide management services, including marketing, recruitment, hiring staff, and professional development.

The non-profit Choice Foundation was asked to open a K–7 school where education and management services were contracted out to Mosaica Education Inc., a for-profit organization that is based in Atlanta and manages seventy charter schools across the nation.

Brigitte T. Nieland, the director of education for the Louisiana Association of Business and Industry, highlighted some of their early plans, such as performance pay for teachers who improve student learning. "They're not bound by collective bargaining the way the old system still is," she said. "They're actually talking about performance pay, performance contracts."

For many educators, politicians, and especially parents, the question was not whether these schools were privately managed but rather that were they working. As Philadelphia schools CEO Paul Vallas put it, borrowing a line from China's former leader Deng Xiaoping, "It doesn't matter whether the cat is black or white," he said. "It's whether it catches mice."

Operating under the mandates of a state takeover and control by a state-appointed School Reform Commission, Vallas implemented a "diverse provider" model as a way of generating internal district competition through school choice—a favorite model of Ownership Society leaders. The choice model was supposed to allow parents whose children were in "failing" or low-performing neighborhood schools to transfer to choice schools, including charters under private management. However, in reality, only parents with the wherewithal to transport their kids across town or those with the knowledge of the limited available options were able to participate in the choice program. This along with often lengthy, personal or complicated application forms represented one more way in which charter schools could choose students rather than students choosing schools. Philadelphia's 196,000-student school district would become the site of the largest experiment in private management of public schools in the entire country and a test case for that model and other interventions sanctioned by the NCLB.

A 2007 Rand Corporation study found that after four years and despite generous funding and an unequal share of the city's public education budget, the privately managed charters were not catching mice. Indeed, they were faring no better than the neighborhood public schools they were supposed to replace. The researchers found that Philadelphia's experiment with privately managed charters "provides no evidence to support private management as an especially effective method of promoting student achievement…"[32]

This despite the extremely favorable deals cut among Philly's EMOs, the state, and the district. The privately managed public schools in Philadelphia were given not only more money and better facilities but other perks as well. Edison, for example, was able to operate on the basis of minimum enrollment guarantees. With such guarantees in place, the EMOs were belying their own claim of competition with "government-run" schools. In the case of Edison, hired by the district in 2002 to run twenty schools with a combined enrollment of 13,000 students, enrollment had been in decline for five years straight. No matter. Edison, because of its close relationship with former Pennsylvania Governor Tom Ridge, had a guaranteed minimum enrollment of 12,591 written into its contract with the state. When enrollment dropped to 10,395 by 2006, the company was paid an extra $1,647,000 for the 2,196 students it wasn't teaching.[33] This while the entire school district was facing a financial shortfall.

Privatization of public school management has raised concerns about its impact on a teaching profession already battered and depleted by the traditional assembly-line system, burnout, and bias against veteran teachers. Despite promises of higher or comparable pay and greater teacher empowerment, the new for-profits are lessening the worth and value of teachers, taking away their collective bargaining rights and turning them into sixteen-hour-a-day clerks or school baristas. Charter school operators often seek to build on a blank slate rather than take on the more difficult job of restructuring existing schools. Though they try to recruit the most competent available teachers, they usually end up hiring younger and therefore lower-paid—albeit more energetic—staff and those who are willing to serve purely at the pleasure of one or another school operator, like the teachers in the ad at the beginning of the chapter, to push that operator's agenda into the classroom. A 2004 study of Delaware's charter schools found that their teachers were younger, more likely to be African-American or Latino, and had a lower percentage of advanced degrees. They also had higher teacher attrition rates.[34]

As charter schools moved from playing small, experimental roles in public school districts to becoming the major strategy for urban school restructuring, they increasingly looked at themselves and their operators as a separate class of schools. Charter school organizations formed to serve as lobbyists, to push legislation, to conduct and publish their own evaluations, and to do their own authorizing. In many states, laws restrict the number of allowable charters or make local school districts the only official chartering agency. When districts push back against the charters, the organizations move to create new legislation. Ironically, states with the lowest levels of scrutiny in allowing for new charters and in which there were no caps on the number of schools are usually described by charter associations as having "strong" charter school laws.

Then there is the question of money. In some districts, the per-student allotment is so low that charter operators decide to move elsewhere. Other cities with more flexible caps and laws become target areas. A city such as Atlanta, for example, became a target for the new charter entrepreneurs. Georgia Lt. Governor Casey Cagle's Charter System Act allowed entire school districts, not just schools, to apply for charter status. It required local systems to pass on more local tax dollars to charter schools for such costs as transportation and food services. Major metro-Atlanta districts have relatively high tax bases, which attract private operators. Fulton, DeKalb, Atlanta Public Schools, and Decatur City, for example, spend more per pupil than the $7,800 national average. Atlanta Public Schools spends $11,881 and Decatur City $13,233, two of the highest amounts in the state. That money follows students from traditional public schools to charter schools.

By 2007, Georgia had sixty charter schools, up from thirty-five two years earlier. Still, Georgia lagged behind other states.

For instance, Florida has 334 charter schools, Arizona 466, and Texas 237. However, their loose laws and big dollar allotments soon had EMOs from around the country flocking to Atlanta and the rest of the peach state. Imagine Schools in Arlington, Virginia, which operates a charter school in north Cobb and another in Marietta, was approved to open two more in Cobb and possibly one in Atlanta. Edison Schools operated Atlanta's Charles Drew Elementary, which is regularly showcased as a charter school success story. Here's a description of Drew from an *Atlanta Journal-Constitution* article:

> The sparkling Drew campus has a golf course view, use of an Olympic-size swimming pool and large numbers of students who test above county and state averages. Built seven years ago by developers and private donors to help revitalize Atlanta's East Lake community, Drew replaced a traditional public school that was among the worst in the city. This year, the company plans to petition to open schools in Fulton, Carroll, Cherokee, Cobb, Douglas, Gwinnett and Paulding county school systems and in the city of Atlanta.[35]

"Companies that manage charter schools will come to Georgia if they believe they can make money," Alex Molnar told the *Journal-Constitution*. Molnar, an Arizona State University education professor, has studied and written extensively on what he would call the charter school industry. "If Georgia's laws are written in a way money can be channeled to corporate entities, it will draw them in," he said. Reaffirming Molar's point, Edison president Lee Nunnery said his team is watching Georgia's charter school evolution. "We're keenly interested to see how it's going to evolve," he said. "Georgia is one of the markets we want to focus on."

In Florida, where a statewide referendum mandated smaller class size in all public school districts, the state responded by mandating small schools and charter schools as "revenue neutral" alternatives to large class size. Though the small schools idea gained some success, especially in attempts to convert many of Florida's huge high schools into smaller learning communities, managed charter schools sprouted like Kudzu across the state.

Legislation in Florida allowed only for charter schools that offered some educational innovation that regular public schools could replicate. However, with Jeb Bush occupying the governor's mansion, privately managed charters flourished, especially in Dade County (Miami) and Hillsborough County (Tampa), and usually without any curricular or instructional innovation that public schools would want to copy. When the for-profit operator Chancellor Academies tried to open two new elementary schools in Pinellas County in 2000, it drew opposition from the NAACP Legal Defense Fund. The Fund argued that Chancellor schools were purposefully racially segregated and that the company made no effort to diversify. Chancellor pulled back its charter application rather than face scrutiny of its student population. Hillsborough's superintendent also expressed concern over how Chancellor's recruitment policies would mesh with the district's court-ordered desegregation plan. The plan, passed by the school board in November, 2000, gives parents greater school choice with the hope that magnet programs and other enticements will attract suburban students to city schools, smoothing racial imbalances. However, for-profit school operators such as Chancellor had no interest in racial balance—quite the opposite.

In Florida, for-profit operators such as Chancellor, which must compete with large national operators such as Edison, rely heavily on student enrollment. In return for managing the school—providing teachers, curriculum, janitorial staff, and administration, among other necessities—the company takes from 12 percent to 20 percent of its state funding, which is based on the number of students enrolled in the school. To increase profit margins, they create larger schools.

When Chancellor proposed to open two new 600-student elementary schools in Hillsborough, it raised the hackles of parents and community groups. "As more states pass charter school laws, we are going to see more privately managed public schools," said Jennifer Morales, a researcher at the university's Center for Education Research, Analysis and Innovation.[36] "The fact that Chancellor wants to open up a very-high-enrollment school raises some concerns," Morales said of Chancellor's planned 600-student schools in Hillsborough. "The business model demands economy of scale in that the companies have to have a certain number of students to keep it cost-effective. You don't want to employ a janitor for 30 kids."

Another concern is that falling enrollments would cause for-profit operators to close schools in poor neighborhoods, often in midyear and without providing options for its remaining students and families. This threat makes one look at Joe Nathan's charter accountability commitment of produce-or-close in a different light.

A charter school in Austin, Texas, run by Charter School Administrative Services of Southfield, Michigan, closed overnight last December after steep enrollment drops. Families were left scrambling to find new schools. KIPP Academy, one of the largest (non-profit) charter school operators, closed schools in Chicago and Denver when they became too difficult or unprofitable to manage.

Though Florida legislators offered charters as an antidote to large class size, the close margins on which charter school operators worked necessitated larger school and class size, a willingness to close low-enrollment schools, and the ability to build profit margins by leveraging real estate or vertically integrating connected businesses (i.e., training providers, advertising, or expensive curriculum-testing packages). They also necessitated the lowest possible labor costs, including the cost (salaries and benefits) of teachers and principals. When you walk into any managed charter school, you're likely to find few, if any, veteran teachers or administrators. That's one of the reasons why charter school associations campaign vigorously against teacher certification rules and for chartering laws that bar teachers' unions.

There are charter schools that are doing a good job of providing innovative and high-quality alternatives to traditional schools. Many of them were among the original group of small schools started by educators and community groups more than a decade ago. The MET in Providence comes immediately to mind. Others, such as Boston's Pilot Schools, though heavily funded by Gates and other power foundations, still see themselves very much as public schools with a public mission and have a working relationship, albeit a rocky one, with the teachers' union.

In Los Angeles, Steve Barr has gone where angels fear to tread, moving aggressively to take over several of L.A.'s enormous, low-performing high schools with his unionized Green Dot chain of charter schools. In the face of strong resistance from a school board, which over the years has seemed immune to any and every reform or restructuring plan, and a hesitant and conflicted superintendent (a former naval officer) on a mission to reform the schools' top-down style, Barr has taken his plan directly to the teachers, offering them higher salaries, better health care plans and, most important, a greater voice in decision making and power over their own teaching.

At John Locke High School in the Watts section of L.A., Barr was able to get a majority of tenured faculty members to sign a petition calling for Locke to secede from the Los Angeles Unified School District (LAUSD) and, under Green Dot management, get their funding directly from the state. Locke, with its 3,400 African-American and Hispanic students and $19 million budget, had become a giant dropout factory. Fewer than 20 percent of incoming Locke students even make it to senior year. Even with an influx of money from the Gates Foundation, money which was initially supposed to lead to small-school restructuring in schools such as Locke, little was done under the previous administration to change the lives of Locke students or its teachers.

Ironically, it was former Colorado Governor Roy Romer who was supposed to lead the reform initiative in this, the nation's second largest school district. After five years of inertia, Romer left to run a $60 million national school reform initiative funded by the Gates and Broad foundations. The new superintendent, former Admiral David Brewer, came into town with his own top-down, strongman plan for reform. Among his first steps was a contract to produce a study that, of course, showed all the horrible failings of the previous administration and promised L.A.'s business community that with their support, he would straighten out the mess left over from Romer's term. Facing a brewing contract battle with the union and rival factions supporting either a mayoral takeover of the schools or keeping power in the hands of the traditional bureaucracy, Brewer and the board were no match for Green Dot's guerilla tactics.

Barr believes that he has the winning model, that there's an organizational-management solution for most of the problems facing L.A.'s humongous high schools. For many teachers, students, and parents, Barr's initiative appears like a rope thrown to a drowning man.

The Green Dot plan has forced the district leadership and the teachers' union to come up with a reform plan of their own. The district's initial response was typical. Locke's principal, Frank Wells, was escorted off the campus by security and relieved of his duties, charged with allowing his teachers to leave their classrooms to collect and sign petitions. Barr had used the traditional tactics of union organizers to organize a critical mass of disgruntled and demoralized teachers. Union president A.J. Duffy would have no choice but to respect the decision of this powerful group of veteran teachers and members of his union. As he told the L.A. Times:

> When a staff gets all the information to make a decision...we would support whatever they want, even if we disagree with it, I understand the teachers' frustrations. The district is not receptive to change and as hard as we have pushed we have not been able to convince them that change is needed. But, I guess they've got the message now.[37]

Barr and Green Dot have shaken things up in L.A. in the way charter schools were meant to do. More important, as they expand into other urban districts, such as New York and Chicago, they will reframe the whole charter school conversation nationwide, especially regarding the role of unions in charter schools.

However, in the final analysis, it will be an engaged community that determines the future of this public education reform and which priority it values the most. In the meantime, charter schools continue to be an arena of struggle. The prospects for charter school growth nationwide seem strong as the demand among parents for good alternatives continues to grow. However, without a clear and strong sense of purpose, without empowered teachers (including collective bargaining right), without constraints on EMOs and CMOs, this growth will do little to improve public school education. Moves to increase the caps on the number of charter schools will continue to be limited until charters are able to deliver better student performance, until authorizers can ensure adequate oversight, and until EMOs are held publicly accountable. This will most likely include some kind of mutually beneficial relationships between charters and the teacher unions.

However, external pressures from conservative philanthropists who contribute heavily to the EMO-run schools could easily override attempts to make charters more accountable and union-friendly. Therefore, it becomes impossible to influence or change charter school policies and politics without dealing with the policies and politics of the foundations that drive them.

4

THE TWO FACES OF PHILANTHROPY: SMALL SCHOOLS ALONG THE FAULT LINES OF WEALTH AND CLASS

The whole people must take upon themselves the education of the whole people and be willing to bear the expenses of it. There should not be a district of one mile square, without a school in it, not founded by a charitable individual, but maintained at the public expense of the people themselves.

—John Adams, U.S. President, 1785

The rise of the Ownership Society has altered the face and function of American philanthropy; nowhere more so than in the field of education and school reform.[1] Foundations, corporate giving programs, and individual private donors have long played a huge role in school reform. However, today that role assumes a disproportionate position, as urban public schools grow more dependent on private grants and donations, not only to finance new initiatives but even to cover basic operating costs of schools.

Giant foundations and corporate mega-funds, such as the Bill and Melinda Gates Foundation and the Eli Broad Foundation, now supply to new educational trends and organizations more than money. Their backing lends a measure of clout, political credibility, and favorable media attention. As the largest foundations control even larger concentrations of private wealth, their power over public institutions grows larger. For example, the Broad Foundation now trains superintendents and district CEOs in the Broad model of leadership and then uses its economic and political clout to inject them at the top of dozens of schools systems, both urban and suburban. As CUNY professor and small-schools activist Michelle Fine told us, "Broad gives large cash awards to several urban school districts and then pressures the runner-ups to accept Broad-trained executives from Wal-Mart or other companies, as their new CEOs."[1]

As for school reform, these mega funds have also become a source of failed top-down reform initiatives and political machinations that have left teachers and school community members high and dry. The Ownership Society has fueled significant changes within the world of philanthropy. Changes in antitrust and taxation policies have nurtured and protected the greatest concentrations of private wealth in U.S. history. Major shifts in markets—especially the ascendancy of younger ventures in the technology sector—have yielded immense profits quickly. This has led to an unprecedented concentration of capital and power, a historic increase in the number of private foundations of all sizes and, most significantly, a handful of exceptionally large private foundations or "power philanthropists," as we call them here. The very presence of these giant funds has shifted more influence and decision making out of the public domain, especially in the arena of public education. It's a power shift that threatens the very existence of public space throughout society.

Says Fine, "We've got to see who's pulling those strings. We need to take back public ownership, public interest, over the schools and the curriculum." The Ownership Society is built on alliances and partnerships that work to influence and control public education and school reform from the top down. These networks are political, financial, social, and ideological; they include think tanks, foundations, political networks, and corporate leaders as well as families.

When a relatively small activist group of neoconservative ideologues took hold of the Department of Education in 2001, they sought to consolidate the Ownership Society agenda by exercising control over the $60 billion K–12 federal education budget to drive state and local spending priorities; they sought also to recruit a growing and increasingly active sector of private educational philanthropists. Others call this sector "corporate philanthropy" or "strategic philanthropy." Frederick Hess of the American Enterprise Institute has aptly dubbed this activist tendency "muscular philanthropy." The group includes a broad spectrum of private funders, large and small, ranging from the Walton Family Foundation, the Milwaukee-based Lynde and Harry Bradley Foundation, on the political Right, to the liberal-moderate Ford, Carnegie, Broad, and Bill and Melinda Gates foundations; some are so big, they consider themselves above traditional political alignments.

They are all key actors on a stage in which urban public schools go begging. Like medical systems in Africa, our urban schools are coming to rely on private funding sources for their very survival. This posture of dependency affords funders such as Bill Gates and Eli Broad, and even much smaller individual and corporate giver, far more power than they should reasonably have in a democratic society. Even publicly elected school boards or officials, bending under the weight of cash shortfalls and pressured by alluring grant opportunities, often shift direction, accept unfavorable conditions, or abrogate traditional agreements, including union relationships, to meet the terms of a funder.

While competing for and accepting private grant support, New York's small schools have found themselves at the mercy of private foundations both large and small, leaving parents, teachers, and community residents virtually excluded from the decision-making process. David Herszenhorn of the *New York Times* describes such an instance, examining the relationship between private donors and the Beginning with Children Charter School, a small school housed in a former factory in Brooklyn. The school made the state's list of high-performing schools thanks to rising reading and math test scores among its black and Hispanic students. The school's founders and wealthy patrons, Joseph and Carol Reich, who have invested hundreds of thousands of dollars into New York charter schools, became disenchanted with the way in which the school was run. The donors then used their contributions as a lever to override educators' decisions about curriculum and instruction. When the Reichs threatened to withdraw their financial "investment" in the school, as if they were selling off a low-performing stock, they forced resignations from the school's governing body. The clash, writes Herszenhorn,

> has exposed fault lines of wealth and class that are perhaps inevitable as philanthropists, in New York and nationwide, increasingly invest in public education, providing new schools to children in poor neighborhoods while making communities dependent on their generosity.[2]

Despite lots of talk in recent years in Congress and state legislatures about accountability, the largest foundations remain virtually unregulated, unaccountable to anyone but their own trustees or, in the case of the Gates and Broad Fund, mainly to Bill and Eli. By 1995, the muscle philanthropists had begun to exert a profound influence on the small-schools movement, using sizeable grants to help move it from the margins to the mainstream of school reform. However, unlike individual charter school "angels" such as the Reichs, the muscle philanthropists exert their controlling influence over entire school districts and over national policy decisions.

Facing huge cuts in local and state education budgets, districts turn to foundation support, which may have seemed benevolent and harmless. The rationale is usually something like, "We'll take the money and use it our way." They soon learn that private funding brings with it pressures that may run counter to many of their own and the reform movement's core values. Getting in line for major grant programs has often required acceptance of top-down mandates, enforced by intermediary organizations, rather than direct communication with the funders, and non-negotiable terms. "Non-negotiable" has in fact become a key word in the lexicon of muscle philanthropy.

In one large urban district in Ohio, non-negotiables included converting each large high school into completely autonomous small schools, each with its own principal. This pure small-school conversion plan, coming from the Gates Foundation and obviously drawn up by paid consultants far from ground zero, looked perfect on paper. However, when it came to pushing it on schools without the leadership capacity or where such a plan ran counter to the experiences of the school community, it was a dead plan walking. Though foundations have every right to leverage their funding to push change and innovation, all change strategies and plans must be negotiable with the school community if they are to have any chance of success.

It's very difficult for the superintendent to turn back a large grant. To do so could bring the criticism that he or she had passed up resources, a charge that could be a career-breaker.

However, the top-down approach and the negative relationships it engenders between school reformers and district educators and between administrators, unions, parents, and community members have caused severe, often irreparable damage. Another Ohio district that we visited gave back its Gates money to evade unpalatable non-negotiables that came along with the small-schools funding. The sad thing was that the school community then associated the idea of smaller learning communities with Gates. The well was poisoned.

In 2004, Secretary of Education Paige moved to defund the federal Smaller Learning Communities (SLCs) initiative to shift some $240 million dollars away from high school restructuring and into support for private and parochial schools. The federal SLC grant offered hope to teachers in large, urban, violence-prone high schools. The SLC grant program had originated in 2000 after Columbine, with strong bipartisan support. Now on the chopping block, the program was saved only after intensive lobbying and congressional trade-offs in a highly contentious and polarized political climate. Several of the largest foundations, including Gates, began advising school districts and departments of education to steer clear of SLCs and concentrate on closing low-performing schools and replacing them exclusively with new start-ups or charter schools. Gates-funded "research" began to shift its line. One report by Gates consultants Fouts & Associates, L.L.C., claimed evidence that differences in school environments "had no clear impact on student learning" and warned that "SLCs can be very disruptive to the school."[3]

Conservative think tanks had long been advising Bush's people that high school restructuring was a wrong-headed strategy: that it was too expensive and too difficult and would have to rely too much on the support of local school bureaucrats and the teachers unions. They were naturally pessimistic about the chances of success of traditional school reform in general, let alone reform that involved basically the same teachers, students, and administrators currently in place. Despite the early positive and promising research coming out of Chicago's decentralized reform initiative, their advice to Paige, a former district administrator and bureaucrat himself, was to cut your losses with the big, conventional high schools and focus instead on creating new privately managed charter schools, rather than wasting time and pouring more money down the restructuring drain.

The near-$2 billion Gates small-schools initiative was much more than a traditional foundation's attempt to push innovation into schools. In 1999, Gates hired the former school superintendent from Federal Way, Washington to run the foundation's $6 billion education program. Vander Ark, like Bill Gates, had been sold on the idea of small schools. He had tried and failed to restructure Federal Way's large (1,600-student) high school, unable to sell the idea to his teachers, their union, and conservative elements within the community.

Vander Ark went about his new assignment, leveraging the foundation's money to create hundreds of new small schools and restructure traditional large high schools, first in the state of Washington and then nationwide. He went on a search for replicable models and found a few external and intermediary organizations and leaders who he felt were capable of driving the process forward. They included the Bay Area Coalition of Equitable Schools, headed by Steve Jubb and charter school guru Joe Nathan at the University of Minnesota's Center for School Change (CSC).

Pointing to "a growing body of research, including University of Washington education Dean Pat Wasley's study of Chicago's small schools movement, that suggested students thrive in smaller academic settings," Vander Ark used $350 million of the fund's money to get the small-schools movement on its feet. The grants, marking the foundation's first gift to schools outside its home state, spanned the country from New York to

Alaska. The biggest—$13.5 million—went to the Providence, Rhode Island school district for work on devising ways to create smaller learning environments and on improving teaching and strengthening community involvement. Nathan's group received $7.9 million to the Cincinnati; St. Paul, Minnesota; and West Clermont, Ohio districts to explore ways to reconfigure ten large high schools serving a total of 16,000 students into smaller learning settings. Other early Gates grant recipients included The Big Picture Co., headed by Dennis Littky and Elliot Washor, cofounders of the path-breaking, progressive MET school in Providence (RI); the Center for Collaborative Education in Boston, whose director, Dan French, would become the driving force behind that city's innovative Pilot schools; and EdVisions, a pioneering teachers' cooperative that ran the Minnesota New Country School in Henderson (MN). EdVisions was tapped to replicate that model with fifteen new schools.

Joe Nathan, CSC's director, told us that there were many ways to approach such a challenge, including splitting up schools within one large building. The first steps, he said, were for parents, teachers, students, and community members to explore options and visit successful sites before agreeing on a plan. However, the foundation, working under Vander Ark's direction, pursued top-down strategies more aligned with Gates' corporate style of leadership than with one of community engagement.

In district after district, the arbitrary goals and timelines of the power-philanthropists clashed with local reform goals and with district leaders, educators, parents, and students. Some of these district leaders had no real desire or capability to implement the Gates model, especially if they had to keep to the foundation's time line. Strict implementation could mean having to handle a revolt on the part of teachers and principals. In some districts such as Cleveland and San Francisco, the threat of a Gates invasion led to the departure of veteran superintendents. On the Gates side, program officers were told to put increased pressure on intermediary organizations, such as KnowledgeWorks in Ohio or the Oregon Small Schools Initiative (OSSI).

VanderArk sought to build new contending power centers in each urban school district, and he had the dollars and political heft behind him to do it. He also had access to mass media and journals in the field to push the foundation's perspective. Just to put the scope of education funding and funding for small schools in perspective, the Gates Foundation's $1.5 billion investment in its small-schools initiative through December 2006 is larger than its malaria ($758 million) and AIDS ($650 million) funding combined.

Gates funding was so large and widespread that it felt as if every initiative in the small schools and charter world were being underwritten by Bill and Melinda. If you wanted to start a school, hold a meeting, organize a conference, or write an article in an education journal, run it by Vander Ark. So it's understandable that small-schoolers were shaken when they first began hearing of shifts in Gates's funding strategy and when stories began appearing in *Education Week* indicating that the foundation's interest in high school restructuring was fading. The foundation that had recently seemed to hold out the greatest help and support for major change efforts now appeared to be lining up behind the Ownership Society line of closing hundreds of urban high schools and turning them over to private management companies.

The first public clue was a June 16, 2004 *Education Week* article by Caroline Hendrie, in which Vander Ark was interviewed extensively. Hendrie wrote:

> As a strategy for reforming secondary education in America, small schools have gotten big. Prodded by an outpouring of philanthropic and federal largesse, school districts and even some states are downsizing public high schools to combat high dropout rates and low levels of student achievement, especially in big-city school systems.

For longtime proponents of small schools, the groundswell of support for their ideas was making for heady times.[4]

Then the other shoe dropped:

Despite the concept's unprecedented popularity, however, evidence is mounting that "scaling up" scaled-down schooling is extraordinarily complex. A sometimes confusing array of approaches is unfolding under the banner of small high schools, contributing to concerns that much of the flurry of activity may be destined for disappointing results. "It's very, very difficult to do this well," said Tom Vander Ark, who heads the Bill & Melinda Gates Foundation's mammoth initiative to create small high schools. "Small is not a panacea. It's a platform that helps you do the things you need to do to help kids succeed." Vander Ark surmised that Gates' reform would have to shift gears. Rather than converting large high schools into smaller learning communities or small schools, said the Gates leader, "we need to close a thousand schools."

Small-schools activists, teachers, and researchers already knew that small schools weren't a "panacea" and that high school restructuring was arduous, demanding work. After all, they had been doing the work for about a decade in most cities. Many suspected that Vander Ark's gloomy assessment of the prospects for high school reform, particularly for the conversion of large high schools, was a reaction to the failed Gates-funded small-schools project at Denver's Manual High School. The Manual project was a top-down attempt at high school restructuring. In a bygone era, Manual had been Denver's flagship black high school. In recent years, the impoverishment of the surrounding community and of Manual's student body, accompanied by a middle-class exodus, had helped to turn Manual into a high-poverty school with an 86-percent poor and minority population, including a growing percentage of Spanish-speaking immigrant students.

The school fell into decline and disrepair. Its problems were those common to low-income schools: a revolving-door series of principals, a shrinking school population, and a shortage of highly qualified teachers. The school was also ill equipped to provide needed services to its new English-language learners. A *Denver Post* story described the plight of one of the long line of Manual principals, Nancy Sutton:

> Sutton tried almost everything to improve Manual: small learning communities, off-campus internships, and group learning. High school reform was still relatively new. "[We were] ahead of the national knowledge base, ahead of what people knew what to do," Sutton said. "I was doing everything, we all were, that I thought was research-based." But teachers felt pulled in different directions...Manual was at the very bottom of all Colorado high schools on the 2000 Colorado Student Assessment Program tests. Sutton and some of her school leaders in 2001 decided to take a stab at one more school reform, applying for a Gates Foundation grant to break up Manual into three small schools. At the time, Gates was investing hundreds of millions of dollars across the country, mostly in urban areas, in small-school reform. These schools were believed to save at-risk students by giving them personal relationships and high expectations. The school board approved Manual's "breakup" in the spring of 2001. Most teachers found out about the plan in April from a note in their mailboxes. They had until August, when school started, to figure it out. "We resented it," said Mario Giardiello, who taught at Manual from 1999 to 2003. "Everything felt like it was being done to us. ...All of this was done without the students' or teachers' input.[5]

With little knowledge or understanding of the unique needs, history, and conditions within the rapidly changing Manual community, the Gates Foundation jumped into the fray armed with a boiler-plate restructuring plan to turn Manual into three completely autonomous schools: Leadership Academy, Arts, and Cultural Studies. Through its intermediary, the Colorado Children's Campaign, Gates pushed its own arbitrary time line for change, propelled in part by a need to quickly identify a national, replicable model for the Foundation's new high school initiative. The Colorado Children's Campaign director, Van Schoales, compared the restructuring to "going into a teenager's room and trying to rearrange it for him."[6] Even besieged principal Nancy Sutton suggested that Manual "provides a model that might work for schools with few resources to make the transformation."[7]

However, in Denver, a resistant district leadership unwilling to cede power to outsiders pushed back. Teachers, feeling left out of the decision-making process, also pushed back. Most important, students, parents, and community groups expressed anger—not so much at the small-schools plan but at the top-down way in which it was being imposed on them. The Gates "model" was never really implemented. Its pure, autonomous small schools soon turned into three amorphous programs, with kids and teachers trying to make up for shortages by crossing over from school to school for needed classes and programs.

Finally, Gates and the district gave up. The funding was pulled. The district announced that Manual would instead be shut down, its kids shipped to schools throughout the city. Teachers lost their jobs. The community lost a precious resource. The results were predictable. As Seymour Sarason has pointed out,

> The problem of change is the problem of power, and the problem of power is how to wield it in ways that allow others to identify with, to gain a sense of ownership of, the process and goals of change. That is no easy task; it is a frustrating, patience-demanding, time-consuming process. Change cannot be carried out by the calendar, a brute fact that those with power often cannot confront. The change process is not engineering one.[8]

Or, as one parent put it, "We aren't against change. We just want it done with us, not to us." A student activist told the media, "We are tired of not being heard and being pushed aside."[10] Another student summed it up this way: "The classes were too big; the course selection was too small. There was too much segregation, too little organization."

The shock waves from the Manual debacle reverberated throughout the small-schools movement, leaving some advocates and Manual teachers in despair: How could something so promising and so well funded turn so sour? Vander Ark concluded that the problem wasn't with the Gates model of change but rather something inherent in high schools such as Manual. In a *Business Week* article, Vander Ark summed up the Manual experience by estimating that up to 20,000 irreparable neighborhood high schools would have to be closed down,[9] a disaster for some communities, potentially on a par with Hurricane Katrina. Restructuring high schools, creating smaller learning communities, working for school change with existing faculties and students, and engaging communities in the process were knocked off the top of the Gates funding agenda.

In Oregon, a $1.4 million Gates small-schools grant to the OSSI had enabled them to draw South Medford High School into their initiative. The well-intended OSSI effort, which included seventeen Oregon schools, sought to increase high school graduation rates and enhance academic performance by engaging Medford teachers in collaborative teaching and creating personalized environments in which teachers can identify and help struggling pupils.

In late November of 2006, North Medford had debuted its freshman academy and was committed to adding sophomores to its academy plan the following fall, in accord with the Gates time line. However, the school was struggling to regain some stability after losing Principal Doug McKenzie and Vice Principal Carolyn Hayes. North Medford administrators decided they would hold off on opening any more schools until fall 2008 after a new administration was put in place. However, when they learned that they were obligated under the Gates grant to open at least one small school next fall, they went ahead anyway without a principal and under pressure from district leaders who feared losing the grant money.[11] When they couldn't move fast enough or deviated in some ways from the "model" and time line set by the foundation and its conduit, the funding was pulled. There was some degree of irony in the situation when one OSSI leader told the school's educators, "We think it's great what [you're] doing to better serve students. But it's different from the original notion and our agreement…"

Here was one more example of school reform wherein the particular conditions at the school were disregarded and an admittedly positive high school reform initiative was sacrificed when it conflicted with the arbitrary time line of the investor foundation. On the bright side, district leaders remained committed to restructuring, with or without Gates money.

When in 2004 the Gates Foundation made its strategic shift, Bill Gates himself, in a speech to the National Governors Association, made his case that American high schools were "obsolete" and "un-reformable." Neither Secretary Paige nor his successor, Spellings, at the DOE could echo Gates' "un-reformable" line, regardless of whether they believed it; instead, they would push for the closings of "failing" or "persistently violent" schools and offer escape routes out of public schools for what they hoped would be thousands of students, to fill the seats in voucher-funded private, parochial, or privately managed charters. This was no grand conspiracy but rather a perfect storm driven by the Ownership Society agenda, with the No Child Left Behind Act as its main political instrument and the muscle foundations as its ally.

The Gates Foundation, on the other hand, presented itself as a more liberal social force and international resource for health care and social services for the poor and for closing the "achievement gap" in public education. Indeed, if not for Bill and Melinda Gates, many underdeveloped countries in Africa would not have nearly the public health systems they possess, and such pandemics as malaria and AIDS would be even worse than they are. Gates alone invested nearly $2 billion dollars in high school reform nationwide. However, the question was rarely asked: why millions of people should be dependent on the generosity of the world's richest man for basic human needs such as health and education.

After Bill Gates decided to come over from Microsoft to run the Foundation directly, a *Los Angeles Times* writer revealed that nearly 95 percent of the Foundation's tax-free funds were being spent on profitable private investments that did great harm to the environment in countries worldwide.[12]

While the Foundation was pouring $218 million into polio and measles immunization and research worldwide, including in the Niger Delta, and while funding inoculations to protect health, its stock portfolio included investments of $423 million in Enid, Royal Dutch Shell, Exxon Mobil, Chevron, and Total of France—the same companies responsible for most of the flares blanketing the Delta with pollution, beyond anything permitted in the United States or Europe.

Gates was far from alone in the Foundation's destructive investment practices. However, many large foundations were engaging in far more socially conscious and ethically consistent investment practices. According to *Times* writer Charles Piller, major foundations that make social justice, corporate governance, and environmental stewardship key considerations in their investment strategies include the Ford Foundation, worth $11.6 billion, the nation's second-largest private philanthropy; the John D. and Catherine T. MacArthur Foundation; the Rockefeller Foundation; and the Charles Stewart Mott Foundation.

Bill Gates had his own complex relationship with Ownership Society leaders. His biggest problem with the feds was a major anti-trust lawsuit during the Clinton Administration. That case was prosecuted by then-Assistant Attorney General Joel Klein, who headed up the Justice Department's anti-trust division. Klein would later become the Chancellor of New York City schools, and his schools would in turn become the recipient of more than $100 million in Gates small-schools grants.

No one is really sure how the case was settled, except that Gates asked for and got a private meeting with Klein in May, 1998 on the eve of the scheduled release of the Windows 98 operating system. House Speaker Newt Gingrich flew to Seattle in 2000, both to raise money and to castigate the Justice Department for its prosecution of Microsoft.[13] Gates had already given more than $200,000 to the RNC. Ultimately, the suit went away, even though the company has since been kept under close watch.

The point here is not that somehow Gingrich or Klein fixed the suit. It may have been that the suit was too complex and unwinnable. However, in the process, new relationships were formed that may have influenced the direction of Gates' funding in the years to come. Whether gratitude and reciprocity played a part is impossible to establish. However, particularly intriguing is this quote from Gingrich's speech, reported by the AP, which more or less defined the role of government in the Ownership Society and foreshadowed the 2007 scandal in the Justice Department over the firing of federal prosecutors. Said Gingrich:

> There are a range of opportunities for the Justice Department other than trying to destroy jobs at one of America's leading companies and trying to weaken America's role in the world market. The purpose of the American government is to strengthen American companies in the world market and increase American exports in the world market, not to undermine American companies.

This new relationship between Gates and the neo-cons might account for the apparent shift in the Gates Foundation's education funding policies, including its shift away from public high school conversions to support of privately managed charter schools.

Nearly a decade after the Microsoft suit, Gates' company was again up against the legal wall after an anti-trust suit filed by competitor Google. Bush-appointed prosecutor Thomas Barnett, who spent a good part of his career working for Microsoft, handled the case this time. Barnett was quick to dismiss Google's claims. The *New York Times* called the case an illustration of "the political transformation of Microsoft, as well as the shift in antitrust policy between officials appointed by President Bill Clinton and by President Bush."[14]

In 2006, the Gates Foundation nearly doubled in size when it merged with Warren Buffet's fund. The lifetime donations of philanthropist Andrew Carnegie, who once said, "The man who dies rich, dies disgraced," came to a comparatively meager $7 billion in today's money.

Thus, the Gates Foundation, thanks to the infusion of $31 billion from Warren Buffett, became larger than the next eight U.S. foundations combined, with annual spending larger than the annual budget of UNICEF. It is now more than five times the size of the $11 billion Ford Foundation. And the $3 billion spent by the Gates Foundation each year nearly doubles the entire $1.66 billion budgeted by the World Health Organization.

Warren Buffett's bequest to the Gates Foundation could pose threats to civil society and philanthropy in ways that people haven't considered, worried political philosopher Benjamin Barber:

> Bundling software and hardware, a kind of monopoly, was a bad thing for Gates' Microsoft. That's why the government sued. Bundling enormous philanthropies might not be that good for Gates' Foundation

either. Big bucks may increase efficiency but will narrow philanthropy's overall diversity, at least for experimentation, for entrepreneurship and for choice. Before we join Warren Buffett and start willing our money to the Gates Foundation, let's remember that diversity is the private market's real virtue. More foundations should be the goal, not bigger foundations.[15]

Buffett's "contribution" to the Gates fund was an oblique statement of support for the Ownership Society. Buffett explained his latest investment with a stinging commentary about the weaknesses of government policy making and action, saying he was likely to get a better bang for his philanthropic buck by selecting what he referred to as the "Tiger Woods of philanthropy" rather than letting government get a share of his wealth.

Critic Rick Cohen took issue with Buffett's remarks in a letter to *Philanthropy Journal*:

Again, big danger sirens ought to sound. As big as the Gates Foundation is or will become, its resources are a pittance compared to the dimensions of the problems it wants to solve—major diseases and extreme poverty, to name just two. Gates and Buffett have to be careful that government doesn't look to the foundation or to philanthropy writ large to supplant necessary government investments in problems and solutions. Already, the Bush administration's fiscal year 2007 budget proposals cited the availability of Gates Foundation moneys as its rationale for cutting its small school program from the Education Department's budget.[16]

Elizabeth Boris, who studies the non-profit sector at the Urban Institute, a Washington think tank, asked, "What kind of accountability is there for them?"[17] After all, a three-person board, made up of Mr. Gates, his wife Melinda, and Mr. Buffett, is running the foundation. However, said Boris, the size of the foundation, which is expected to give away $3 billion a year by 2009, could raise questions about whether philanthropic boards should face new standards for their size and diversity, and whether greater government oversight was required.

While the DOE in part used Gates funding as a rationale to cut the SLC budget, many local school districts already had their eyes set on the prize—a Gates small-schools grant—often used to supplant holes in district operating budgets and keep teacher or administrative positions from being cut, in exchange for the promise of strict adherence to the Gates restructuring model and time line.

The muscle foundations have become driving influences, pushing the reform movement in its current direction, which is away from high school restructuring and teacher, parent, and community engagement and toward "scaling up" replicable models and other replication strategies limited to new-start schools and privately managed charters. Throughout this period, a parallel funding track has also been expanding. Walton and upstart education entrepreneurs such as the New Schools Venture Fund provide start-up and training money for hundreds of privately managed charter schools while offering extra support to the think tanks and to ideological leaders to build a center-right coalition of charter school organizations. Their purpose is to raise the funds and provide political leverage on such issues as charter caps (laws limiting the number of charter schools) and charter school autonomy. Foundations would also fund their own evaluations to "prove" that the charters, as a group or class, were outperforming other public schools.

Since its creation in 1962, Wal-Mart has produced a fortune of more than $100 billion for founder Sam Walton and his family. With the five senior members of the Walton family tied for fourth place in *Forbes* magazine's most recent list of the "400 Richest Americans" (one of the five, John Walton, died in a plane crash in 2005), the Walton's are the richest family in the world, worth more than $100 billion altogether. Though the Walton's have so far largely escaped public scrutiny or much media criticism, an article posted on the homepage of the National Committee for Responsive Philanthropy documents the Walton's propensity for union-busting and love of cheap labor and compares the family to "robber barons" of nineteenth-century America—"the ostentatiously wealthy and corrupt capitalists who dominated the U.S. economy."[18]

Five years before his death in 1987, Walton established the Walton Family Foundation. When his son John took over the fund in 1998, the Walton Family Foundation was funding its education agenda at $4.7 million. By 2004, the foundation gave two-thirds of its $101 million in grants—$66 million—to K–12 schooling, outpacing the educational philanthropy of Ford, Carnegie, Kellogg, and other venerable foundations. Only the Bill and Melinda Gates Foundation gave more to K–12 education.[19]

Most of the fund's giving is in support of "school choice," from charter schools to private school vouchers and tuition tax credits, policies obviously in line with OS budgetary priorities. The foundation's charter school financing has also led others to contribute to the charter cause. Walton funding "was a catalyst for others to give," Donald Fisher, the billionaire founder of The Gap and an active charter school philanthropist who contributes heavily to the KIPP charter school network, told *Philanthropy* magazine in 2005.

> Some critics argue that it is the beginning of the "Wal-Martization" of education, and a move to for-profit schooling, from which the family could potentially financially benefit," says the NCRP. "John Walton owned 240,000 shares of Tesseract Group Inc. (formerly known as Education Alternatives Inc.), which is a for-profit company that develops/manages charter and private school as well as public schools. Although there is nothing wrong with a company or family

trying to make money, using the nonprofit sector to do so is another matter," says the NCRP.

According to *The Nation* magazine writer and researcher Liza Featherstone, Walton's education gifts have a "free market" tilt and fund advocacy groups promoting conservative school "reform"—otherwise known as privatization—such as the Center for Education Reform and the Black Alliance for Educational Options, run by one-time civil rights activist, now conservative voucher advocate, Howard Fuller.

The Walton Family Fund (WFF) is now the single largest source of funding for the voucher and charter school movement. Walton funding, according to Featherstone, "allows some charter schools to spend more per pupil than 'competing' public schools." The ironic result is that though these projects are supposed to demonstrate to the public the wonders of a marketized approach to education, the WFF's money gives its grantees an advantage over other schools, allowing them to perform better than they would otherwise. "[The Waltons] claim to support competition and the free market," says Paul Dunphy, a policy analyst for Citizens for Public Schools, a Boston-based coalition, "but actually they are manipulating the market, conferring advantage on their pet projects."

Walton and Gates conduits include the California-based New Schools Venture Fund (NSVF), launched in 1998 to support private and not-for-profit, charter management companies. Within nine years, the NSVF had raised $100 million, underwriting the work of sixteen EMOs with 102 charter schools serving nearly 30,000 students. By 2010, it expects those numbers to climb to 60,000 students in 200 schools, making it one of the largest charter school funders. By far, the largest NSVF contributor is the Gates Foundation. It committed $30 million in 2006, bringing to $57 million its total giving to the fund. Other contributors include the Los Angeles-based Broad Foundation, the Annie E. Casey Foundation in Baltimore, and the WFF.

Though Fund leaders see themselves as both competitors and supporters of public schools, the Fund's support for EMOs as opposed to the seeding of individual schools is clearly aimed the erosion of public school-district power and undercutting the influence of teachers unions in urban districts such as Chicago, New York, the San Francisco Bay Area, Philadelphia, and Washington, D.C. The big target for the NSVF and for all the muscular philanthropists is post-Katrina New Orleans, the new Mecca for the EMOs.

For the new education entrepreneurs of the Ownership Society, charter-school management is only a piece of the puzzle. Though the actual management of public schools may offer only narrow profit margins, control of school budgets offers more lucrative opportunities for connected supplementary service providers.

"Charters are only part of our strategy," said Ted Mitchell, former president of Occidental College and the Fund's CEO. "Our basic purpose in the world is to support educational entrepreneurs, where entrepreneurship can be helpful in transforming school systems."[20]

Those entrepreneurial endeavors include companies such as New Leaders for New Schools. This company, which began as a project at Harvard's Business School to provide a new corps of leaders for urban public schools, has become almost exclusively a charter-school provider, being steered off course by the power funders, who include entrepreneur Kim Smith and venture capitalists L. John Doerr and Brook Byers, both longtime partners at Kleiner, Perkins, Caufield & Byers, a Silicon Valley firm. Mr. Doerr has helped to direct venture dollars to technology companies, including Google, and has been a major contributor to the Democratic Party.

Prominent neo-con "research" groups such as the American Enterprise Institute, the Heritage Foundation, and the Manhattan Institute, which claim to be doing unbiased research, are also Ownership Society proponents and have been solid backers of both department of education spending on privatization and of Walton's funding strategies. Top policy analysts at these groups have written newspaper opinion pieces around the country supporting Wal-Mart, defending the company in committees in Washington. However, the groups and their employees and consultants have failed to disclose their ties to the giant discount retailer. They have maintained that donations from the foundation have no influence over their research, which is deliberately kept separate from their fund-raising activities.

> However, according to a pair of *New York Times* writers, financing, which totaled more than $2.5 million over the last six years, according to data compiled by GuideStar, a research organization, raises questions about what the research groups should disclose to newspaper editors, reporters or government officials.[21]

The conservative research groups claim that as their mission is to be an advocate for free market policies and less government intrusion in business, it's only natural that Walton would fund them. "Those aims are pro-business, so it's not surprising that companies would be supporters of our work," Khristine Brookes, a spokeswoman for the Heritage Foundation told the *Times* writers.

In New Jersey, a lawsuit to apply state public education funding toward private-school tuition was bankrolled by Wal-Mart and Amway. Amway's Betsy and Dick DeVos, whose multibillion-dollar family fortune is based on Amway sales, directed hundreds of thousands of dollars to conservative activists in Florida, Michigan and elsewhere. Betsy DeVos also sits on the board of the Arizona-based Alliance for School

Choice, the venerable leader of the school-voucher movement and an ally of Excellent Education for Everyone (or E3).

E3, the state's leading proponent of school vouchers, was granted at least $1.65 million from the WFF, which a New Jersey reporter describes "as a perennial underwriter of 'family values' think tanks, Christian schools and Republican candidates for national public office."[22] E3 also has reaped at least $230,000 from the Morristown-based William E. Simon Foundation, whose stated mission is "to strengthen the free-enterprise system and the spiritual values on which it rests: individual freedom, initiative, thrift, self-discipline and faith in God."[23]

The Gates Foundation had its own mantra for schools and was searching for replicable models. Its mantra was the three Rs: "Rigor, Relevance and Relationships." Nobody was quite clear what rigor meant or which MBA over at the Foundation had come up with the term. The dictionary definition of *rigor* was packed with horrible meanings that nobody would want for their own children:

> Strictness or severity, as in temperament, action, or judgment.
> A harsh or trying circumstance; hardship.
> A harsh or cruel act.
> Medicine: Shivering or trembling, as caused by a chill.
> Physiology: A state of rigidity in living tissues or organs that prevents response to stimuli.
> Obsolete stiffness or rigidity.[24]

Relevance to what? What kind of relationships? When taken as another education cereal-box jingle, it really doesn't matter. With Gates's top-down reform model, school personnel would soon learn to repeat the mantra, often and with feeling, if they wanted to get funding.

5

THINK TANKS: THE BRAINS OF THE OWNERSHIP SOCIETY

If the venture philanthropists are the sugar daddies of the Ownership Society, the conservative think tanks are its brain trust. They have provided the intellectual muscle to power school privatization plans from vouchers to for-profit management of public schools and are the leading strategists on the right flank of school reform. Their credibility in the small-schools and charter world is based on their ability to combine their free market and privatization lingo with a critique of bureaucracy and their capture of the language of choice. However, these think tanks were also the ones that made the case that reforming public education, especially large urban high schools, was too difficult an enterprise to pursue and that thousands of school closures and free market solutions were the only worthwhile reforms.

This line of thinking and the politics behind it did great damage to the small-schools movement and were responsible for funding shifts in the federal budget, away from school restrucuring and toward private and charter school support. The right-wing think tanks were also responsible for generating the research base for exclusively phonics-based reading programs and other politically driven curricular mandates.

Unlike many of the more liberal, university-based think tanks, the right-wing tanks are not constrained by any academic standards such as peer-review and usually produce research that matches the political bent of a handful of rich and powerful funders. However, this freedom from academic checks and balances also give the think tanks a certain vitality and popular approach to education politics not often found, for example, in colleges of education. Blogs, Wikis, and Web sites replace liberal academic journals read by nobody outside the field and few in the field.

As far back as 1984, moderate Republican John Saloma was warning of a "major new presence in American politics," by which he meant the emergence of a web of right-wing think thanks and foundations, several of them connected with far-right fringe or neo-fascist movements. If left unchecked, he predicted, "the new conservative labyrinth" would pull the nation's political center sharply to the right.[1]

These emerging think tanks enjoyed close ties, strong influence, and easy entree to the Reagan White House and, later, to the two Bush regimes, but they stayed mainly out on the margins of public school policy arena.

With early backing from the likes of Colorado beer magnate Joseph Coors and leadership from conservative activists such as Paul Weyrich, founding president of the Heritage Foundation, and Lynne Cheney, now a fellow of the American Enterprise Institute (AEI), this early collection of extremist ideologues and cultural warriors would soon move into the catbird seat of conservative politics wherein they sought to improve their positions as shapers of education policy.

Lynne Cheney ascended to the chair of the National Endowment for the Humanities (NEH) as a Reagan appointee in 1986. She still rules the NEH roost today, though no longer from an official position. At first, she favored abolishing the agency altogether, because she considered it to be a tool of the "cultural lefts." Once in charge, however, Cheney stymied grants for research and curricular development addressing multicultural studies, race, or even topics such as the Mafia, which might reflect critically on U.S. history. Cheney explained in a 2003 CNN interview that she wished to promote, "American history that's taught in as positive and upbeat a way as our national story deserves."[2] It was in that ideological pursuit that she torpedoed the work of the prestigious NEH-funded national panel on U.S. history standards, destroying them rather than allowing adoption of a set of standards in which slavery, discrimination, or poverty reared their ugly heads. Weyrich of the Heritage Foundation bragged, "We are different from previous generations of conservatives...We are no longer working to preserve the status quo. We are radicals, working to overturn the present power structure of this country."[3]

This "radical" approach originally included blowing up (metaphorically speaking, of course) the public school system, which to Weyrich and others represented just one more form of governmental control and interference. However, later, as the new radicals found a receptive base of support within the Bush White House and the Congress, they put their own early reform initiatives such as school vouchers on the back burner in exchange for the more profitable and politically viable reform program—privatization of public school management and outside service provision. The questions of whether public schools could be reformed or whether a completely privatized system was needed remained an issue for internal think tank debate. Many of the Ownership Society radicals try to keep up a reformer's front but think the worse-the better when it comes to public education.

Conservative think-tanker William Bennett exemplifies the born-again radicalism of the neo-cons. Since leaving his post as secretary of education under Regan and drug czar under the senior Bush, he has gone full-steam into the virtual charter school business, pulling in millions of dollars in grants from his old cronies at the Department of Education and millions more in contracts from school districts. In Chicago, Bennett's K–12 Inc. virtual school was given a hard-to-come-by charter and a fat contract, without having to jump through the normal chartering hoops. Remember, Bennett was the one who came through Chicago during the Reagan administration, as funding for public education was being drastically cut, only to announce that this district was "the worst in the nation."

When a former Federal Communications Commission member asked him for help in getting legislation passed to pay for Internet access in every public school classroom, Bennett reportedly refused. According to the commissioner:

> He told me he would not help because he did not want public schools to obtain new funding, new capacity, new tools for success. He wanted them to fail so that they could be replaced with vouchers, charter schools, religious schools, and other forms of private education.[4]

The influence of these institutions has now gone well beyond advising on policy issues. Think tanks have effectively repositioned the boundaries of the school reform policy discussion. They've redefined key concepts, such as choice, accountability, achievement gap, and charter schools. Through the constant repetition and dissemination of Ownership Society policy ideas, they have provided philosophical undergirding for privatization, union busting, and the erosion of public space and democracy. They have provided ideological muscle to the conservative educational agenda in times of need.

Heritage's Weyrich attributes the ascendancy of the conservative movement to what he calls "the four M's: mission, money, management and marketing."

"I make no bones about marketing," said the AEI's former president, William Baroody: "We pay as much attention to the dissemination of the product as we do to the content. We're probably the first major think tank to get into the electronic media."[5]

The think tanks are the conservatives' idea-marketing machines. According to a report from National Council for Responsive Philanthropy:

> The Hoover Institution maintains an active public affairs office which links it to 900 media centers across the United States and 450 media outlets abroad. The Reason Foundation, a national public policy research organization that also serves as a national clearinghouse on privatization, has developed an aggressive communications strategy, resulting in 359 television and radio appearances and over 1500 print-media citations in national newspapers and magazines in 1995 ... The Manhattan Institute has held over 600 forums or briefings for journalists and policymakers on multiple public policy issues and concerns, from tort reform to federal welfare policy. And the National Center for Policy Analysis reports that "NCPA ideas" have been discussed in 573 nationally syndicated columns and 184 wire stories over the twelve years of its existence.[6]

From war planning to school privatization, think tanks like the Heritage, Hoover, and Fordham Foundations; American Enterprise and Manhattan Institutes, have all been strategic partners, planners, and researchers for each conservative regime since the 1970s. Not all think tanks are part of a big conservative conspiracy, and there are many differences among them as they compete for funding, political stature, and connections. Nor is it fair to assume that everyone associated with a think tank is a tool of the neo-cons. Several progressive policy wonks write for the far-right AEI and Fordham, lending these institutions an air of objectivity. But with an examination of their roles during the past three decades—years marked by the rise of the neo-conservative movement—it is fair to say that the right-wing network of think tanks have become something other than the laboratory for "scientifically proven" educational and social theories they are cracked up to be.

With nearly $50 million in private funding behind them, their net effect has been to narrow, not broaden, the policy debate. $50 million may not seem like a lot of money for such important research institutions until you realize that the entire annual economics budget at the National Science foundation is less than $20 million. This means that a small group of conservative multi-millionaires can underwrite an impressive array of research institutes and foundations that can in turn market, disseminate, and lend an aura of academic credibility to programs that could never pass muster in most academic institutions. From the fields of economics to education, from the "trickle-down" and "supply-side" economics of the Reagan era to today's phonics-based reading and DIBELS (Dynamic Indicators of Basic Early Literacy Skills) assessment strategies, the conservative think tanks have had only to add the words "research based" to get their political agenda across.

They have also developed local counterparts to push business models and privatization plans in urban districts. One example is Chicago's Civic Committee, which often plays the role of local think tank, producing studies and policy papers that support conservative business strategies. Another is the Mackinac Center for Public Policy in Michigan, a well-funded group of school privatization and free market advocates focused on the state's smaller districts. Whether on education or national security, they project a narrative of national disaster and an image of a public education system so buried in crisis and dysfunction that reform isn't possible and only top-down authority, weakening of civil liberties, and the most extreme privatization measures can save them.

The crisis narrative at times takes the form of pseudo-patriotism, sticking up for America in its international competition with other countries in the global economy, which are trying to take jobs that once belonged exclusively to "us." This version of history omits the role played by many of these same public education critics in the creation of this global economy. Nor is there any mention of many ways in which they have profited from the technological revolution that enables them to do business anywhere on the globe and move to wherever the cost of doing business is cheapest, including the cost of labor. This technology revolution is centered here in the United States, despite our supposedly failing school systems. This revolution was pioneered by the likes of Bill Gates—himself a college dropout who declared American high schools to be "obsolete"—and other members of this new class of billionaire entrepreneurs.

Gates and his Microsoft Corporation have made great use of the right-wing think tanks. Back in 1999 when the company was facing massive anti-trust suits, Gates hired the Independent Institute to run a full-page ad in the *New York Times*. The ads included a letter signed by hundreds of academic "experts" and took on the image of a scholarly report showing how the government had gone overboard in its case against the company. It turned out that Microsoft had not only paid for the ads but was in fact the single largest donor to the Independent Institute, a conservative organization that has been a leading defender of the company since it first came under fire from federal prosecutors.

For the early small-schools movement, the role of the think tanks was murky and complicated. There was a tacit assumption that the educational think tanks, along with their funders, whatever their differences, were after the same thing—real reform of a system badly in need of reform. That's because certain of these policy organizations—the Manhattan Institute is a foremost example—played a critical role at times in exposing bureaucratic mismanagement and corruption within the New York City school system. A few progressive educators such as Seymour Fliegel and Coleman Genn were affiliated with the Manhattan Institute. Fliegel and Genn in particular were instrumental in supporting the fledgling small-schools movements in New York and Chicago. Fliegel's book, *Miracle in East Harlem*,[7] helped put New York's early small schools on the national map, with its portrait of Deborah Meier's pioneering work at Central Park East.

Genn, the superintendent of New York Community School Board 27, became a public hero for wearing a wire to expose corrupt and racist hiring practices on the part of school board members. Genn also managed three small alternative schools in East Harlem and advised our early small-schools movement in Chicago, helping it to navigate the rough waters of the Chicago school bureaucracy.

Fliegel's book would become a handy tool for the neo-cons, however, in their push for vouchers and privatization, the farthest thing from the minds of Meier and her dedicated band of public school teachers at CPE. The Manhattan Institute would later become a central opponent of affirmative action and desegregation plans and a promoter of racial and genetic social theories, like those offered in Institute fellow Charles Murray's *The Bell Curve*.[8]

The basic premise of *The Bell Curve* is that intelligence is largely the property of certain races, especially whites and Asians, who form a "cognitive elite," whereas African-Americans and Latinos as a whole are generally intellectually inferior. To Murray and fellow think-tanker Richard Hernnstein, attempts to highly educate these inferior races was a waste of time and money, as was any attempt to reform public school systems with this end in mind. These racist ideas merged handily with the premise that intelligence could be accurately measured with standardized tests, across racial, language, and national boundaries. Together they formed the cornerstones of conservative educational philosophy and a powerful influence on think-tank policy recommendations.

Early on, the Manhattan Institute saw small schools mainly as proto-charters, whereas Meier and other New York educators saw them as vehicles for democratic, public engagement and teacher empowerment. This distinction, though subtle in the early 1990s, would become significant just a few years later. Fliegel and the Manhattan Institute have now themselves become charter school operators, as have several other think tanks. The Institute has its own affiliated educational management organization (EMO), called the Center for Educational Innovation, which has receives tens of millions of dollars from the Department of Education, over and above its state per-pupil allotment.

The think tanks help to steer billions of dollars in federal, state, and private funding to their politically aligned and connected agencies, EMOs, and service providers. They do that while cutting out most progressive, liberal academic or left-leaning school reform agencies and organizations that could provide professional development, coaching, and support for school restructuring.

William Simon, president of the conservative Olin Foundation, argues that businesses who donate indiscriminately to universities are "financing their own destruction." He asks, "Why should businessmen be financing left-wing intellectuals and institutions which espouse the exact opposite of what they believe in?"[9]

Progressives and even politically neutral or ambivalent reform groups found themselves pegged as "dirtbags" by conservative

DOE leaders such as Reading First Director Chris Doherty, who accused non-aligned reading-literacy experts of trying to "crash our party." Doherty, with support from the conservative think tanks, shoved to the margins many of the agencies that provided valuable support to teachers in the area of literacy, including well-respected university-based reading organizations.

On the other side, progressive educators and reformers were late in supporting their own public intellectuals and policy experts in the field of education reform. It was only in the last few years that progressive funders such as George Soros began establishing think tanks of their own, such as the Open Society Institute. It remains to be seen whether, even under a Democratic administration, they can transcend the top-down style of work and the strong-arm philosophy of change that usually goes hand in hand with heavily funded think tanks. It also remains to be seen whether or not the progressive policy groups and think tanks can break through the hegemony of the Ownership Society think tanks.

Paul Krugman, referring to the Bush administration's "trademark incompetence," wrote: "In appointing unqualified loyalists to key positions, Mr. Bush was just following the advice of the Heritage Foundation, which urged him back in 2001 to "make appointment decisions based on loyalty first and expertise second."[10]

The Fordham Foundation has played a key—if controversial—role in the development of administration education policy. Fordham, led by Chester "Checker" Finn, a George H.W. Bush-era assistant secretary of education, includes other former DOE senior leaders, such as former Secretary of Education Rod Paige; former assistant secretaries of education Diane Ravitch and Bruno Manno; and senior DOE staffer Mike Petrilli. There is easy flow between the DOE and the think tanks and among the tanks themselves. Finn, Fordham's president and senior fellow at Stanford's Hoover Institute, is hardly a neo-con ideologue;

rather, he is much more the right-wing pragmatist. His role as an administration outsider now gives him and the other think-tankers more room to maneuver than he would have at the helm of the Department, wherein Bush administration staffers are measured mainly by their loyalty and willingness to carry out the party line.

Finn thought nothing of trying to beat down an opponent over differences on the No Child Left Behind (NCLB) Act and then reversed his position on the issue with no apologies to those he had previously savaged. He led an ad hominem attack on Jonathan Kozol, a vocal critic of NCLB, impugning Kozol's motives for opposing the law:

> Kozol has grown wealthy by selling books to educators and speaking at their conferences. Now he's joining—even seeking to lead—the anti-NCLB backlash among educators, all the while waving his familiar flag of racism and injustice, yet refusing to offer any plausible alternatives for fixing our failing urban schools.[11]

However, by the following February, as the wind began to shift and administration ratings plummeted, Finn and Petrilli themselves began openly attacking the NCLB and the DOE leadership in the conservative *National Review*. In a critique that would do Kozol proud, Finn and Petrilli wrote:

> The future the commission depicts gives Washington yet more power over the nation's schools; its summary recommendations use the word 'require' (often followed by the word "states") at least 35 times. By contrast, we found just half a dozen "allows" or "permits." Seems the panel is six times more interested in issuing new federal mandates than providing flexibility to states, districts or schools.[12]

Had Finn and Petrilli joined Kozol's anti-NCLB crusade? Finn and his Fordham colleagues, masters of conflicts-of-interest politics, personally helped to bridge the gap between Reaganism (government is bad) and Bushism (government is useful). When the Reading First scandal broke in 2006, Finn and Petrilli leaped to the defense of fallen Reading First director Doherty, blaming instead Secretary of Education Spellings for not standing behind Doherty's borderline criminal activities. Research-tested, phonics-based reading programs were a matter of principle, they argued, and Doherty shouldn't have taken the fall for using any means necessary to ensure the victory of phonics in the reading wars, over the whole-language or blended-reading crowds. Finn even boasted that he, like Doherty, had stacked grant review panels in his days as assistant secretary, using his political cronies rather than experts in the field. Finn wrote,

> When I was an assistant education secretary back in the late medieval period, I spent perhaps a third of my time selecting peer reviewers and panels that had a fighting chance of doing things differently, doing things right—and doing things the way I thought they should be done. Staying out of the legal rough, sure, but absolutely not hitting down the middle of the fairway. That's why I was there.[13]

Finn claims that the peer review process has:

> evolved [into] extensions of the presidential appointee who heads the agency...It is altogether reasonable for him (Doherty) to select reviewers who share his values, his instincts, his convictions, and his hunches. In this sense, the peer-review process is necessarily and properly "political."

For Finn, peer review had evolved into political cronyism, and well it should. "So far as I can tell," wrote Finn, "that's exactly what the much-abused Reading First team did, too. Hoorah for them."

Finn and Fordham typify many of the conservative think tanks in positioning themselves as both policy advisors and direct beneficiaries of the policies they advocate. In the realm of privately managed charter schools, Fordham and Finn acted as early advocates, charter school authorizers and, finally, as operators themselves of a chain of Ohio charter schools. Finn was a founding partner in Edison Schools, Inc. but had no compunction about advocating policies that would directly benefit Edison and other for-profit EMOs. Such is the character of think-tank pragmatism.

Finn and other conservative think-tankers easily made the shift from vouchers to charter schools as their new privatization strategy, whereas many others remained in the voucher camp. In a speech to a group at Harvard University, Finn describes charter schools this way:

> Charter schools are probably the most visible and widespread example of the "marketplace paradigm" of education reform, which basically seeks to "bust up" the current K–12 system and create alternatives, options, and competition that people can access through the marketplace.[14]

Only in passing does Finn even mention teachers in the overall perspective and, of course, he and the rest of the right-wing think tanks oppose teachers' collective bargaining rights and have managed to keep the nation's 4,000 charter schools virtually union-free. Indeed, when it came to a badly needed financial bailout of Washington, D.C. private Catholic schools, the Fordham Foundation's Mike Petrilli, a Finn protégé, came up with a plan. Writing on the foundation's Gadfly blog, this former official of the U.S. Department of Education calls for the conversion of urban Catholic schools into publicly funded charter schools, comfortably blurring the church/state barrier.[15]

Faced with such a formidable, well-funded conservative network operating against public school reform and pushing privatization, what can progressive educators, small-school activists, teachers' unions, and reformers offer as an alternative? What kind of new coalitions need to be built and who will lead them? Those are the difficult questions we take up in Chapter 6.

6

ALTERNATIVES TO TOP-DOWN REFORM

The most effective response to top-down reform is for teachers, parents, and communities to act together powerfully. Real reform is not confined just to the policy arena but, more often, is generated by the way in which educators engage one another and the students they are teaching.

Recently, we read about a so-called turnaround school in an urban district, where the principal was touted as a "superstar" for increasing test scores for two years running. When asked what his "secret" was, the principal replied, "Small groups and plenty of planning time." However, in today's environment, where Ownership Society reform is often anti-teacher or teacher-proof, the superstar's gift to the teachers assumes a rare quality that approaches the revolutionary. The point is that real change requires a high level of engagement, from teachers, parents, students, and the entire school community. Top-down reform, currently being promoted by several big-city mayors and venture philanthropists, is not only undemocratic but ineffective as well.

Early small schools were known for their aura of professional community: that is, teachers acting and working as professionals rather than as assembly-line workers, much the way a team of lawyers, architects, or surgeons works. In many—if not most—of our large, comprehensive high schools, teachers now work in relative isolation. They haven't the time or the resources for effective collaboration, as is done in other professions. Privatization and contractor-run schools, despite their claims of professional community, have only made matters worse, as time spent out of the classroom is often viewed by school managers as unproductive down time, and teachers in such schools generally have no union rights.

When there is time for planning and professional development, teachers may have little control over how that time will be used. Whether in large, traditional public schools or in many small or charter schools, teacher time is managed from the top, especially in those schools wherein curriculum is scripted and professional development is "training" rather than engagement.

There is plenty of evidence to show that the real potential for smaller learning communities lies in their ability to engage teachers as professionals who can reshape their own professional development and use of planning time.[1] A compact faculty size (e.g., a staff of fifteen to twenty for a school of 300) can better support close, interpersonal relationships among faculty members. In such settings, professional development is often enhanced by teaming and by small, task-oriented group formations.[2] For instance, teacher teams may work on interdisciplinary units or on personalized learning plans for all students. Under these circumstances, the entire team, including guidance personnel and even career service staff, share students and may teach multiple subjects or mixed grade levels or collaborate on interdisciplinary teams. In this way, the necessity and opportunities for shared professional learning are increased. In our own work with urban high schools, we have found that the flexible scheduling and opportunities for faculty teamwork in smaller schools allows for a level of depth and an interdisciplinary approach that provide students with a much richer educational experience.

It's one thing for teachers to have time and outside support. It's quite another thing for them to be able to use that time productively, to work in collaborative teams that span grade levels and departments, to facilitate their own professional-development activities, to examine their own and their colleagues' teaching, and to look at student work together. Teachers can take several approaches to this kind of interactive work. One of the most popular and effective is called Critical Friends Groups (CFGs). CFGs are professional learning communities consisting of approximately eight to twelve educators who come together voluntarily at least once a month for about two hours. Group members are committed to improving their practice through collaborative learning. In 1994, the Annenberg Institute for School Reform designed a different approach to professional development, one that would be focused on the practitioner and on defining what will improve student learning. Organizations such as the National School Reform Faculty, based at the Harmony Education Center in Bloomington, Indiana, coach hundreds of teachers to use the CFG protocols.

CFGs are just one example of a break from top-down models that script teachers and are used by many of the EMO-run charter schools to compensate for their lack of experienced, certified teachers and their high turnover rates. CFGs and similar Teacher-Talk groups are designed to empower teachers and rely heavily on teacher wit and personalization of instruction, and knowledge of the student, rather than standardization and teaching to the test.

The underlying principal of small school creation is civic engagement. It's not that teachers and parents need to reject all models or all notions of replication of successful projects. Rather, it's about keeping initiative in their own hands rather than having reform done to them. The metaphor that comes to mind is making the road by walking, which we took from the title of a book of interviews with Myles Horton and Paulo Freire.[3] As every child, community, and school is unique in many ways, local decision making and classroom-based professional development, combined with trust in skilled teachers, trumps what Freire called "the banking system of education." That is to say, there's emerging vision of where we were going but also a meaningful, practical, and immediate task at hand—that of creating or transforming schools.

Many schools and teacher organizations are finding ways to reframe Ownership Society policies, such as performance pay, and turn them into supports for teachers working in the toughest situations and away from simply being de-professionalizing, piece-work, or cost-cutting solutions to educational problems. Of course, these tactical shifts are not worth much without a plan for adequate funding for public education, including a shift away from reliance of property taxes as a primary school funding source.

We recently saw an example of this contradiction between top-down reform and the funding necessary to support it, commonly called *unfunded mandates*. After a year of pushing, Florida's conservative legislature and governor were finally able to force a plan for performance pay on reluctant school districts. Obviously Florida, like most southern states, doesn't have the strongest teacher unions in the world. However, when push came to shove, that same legislature and governor decided that they didn't want to pay the price for victory, so turned around and slashed the $150-million allocation needed to pay for the plan. Performance pay, like so many other top-down reforms, turned out to be a political wedge issue, not a substantive plan to increase accountability or improve teacher pay.

What can be done to create alternatives to disempowering, uninspiring, top-down reform models? Public school parents, educators, and community activists all have to deal with the difficult problems associated with reform, such as making sure we're not merely recreating the present system's inequities and the current two-tiered system of schooling and such as ensuring we're not just changing the organizational structure and management of schools but changing teacher practice and student learning outcomes as well. Finally, we have to keep our guard up lest school reform become a shill for opportunistic school profiteers, without closing off avenues of genuine support from the business and philanthropic sectors. It's a fine line, and it demands a nuanced, agile approach grounded in real experience in changing schools.

Authentic, enduring school reform is impossible without teacher leadership, strong community partnerships, and broadened civic capacity. Add to that the worthy endeavor of saving, and transforming public schools cannot be accomplished short of confronting what Seymour Sarason has described as the complex "behavioral and programmatic regularities" that define school culture.[4] Finally, there has to be a meeting ground between the means and ends of reform; in other words, if we want democratic schools, we need a democratic process of community engagement, a mix of top-down and bottom-up. This requires new, inclusive reform coalitions that are inclusive of parents, educators, students, community residents, teacher unions, small-schools and charter advocates, and allies from the business and philanthropic communities.

Top-down reform, managerial changes, even small schools, are no cure-all for what ails urban public schools. The crisis faced by schools didn't originate in the schools and can't be resolved within the schoolhouse. A plan for reshaping public education cannot be crafted in a vacuum, separate from the rebuilding of neighborhoods and the revitalization of local economies with the creation of jobs, public works, and expanded opportunity. As critical observers such as Jonathan Kozol and Richard Rothstein persist in reminding us, the crisis that affects the schools is in large part a crisis of inequalities not confined to the schools. Issues around access to health care, to employment, to decent and affordable housing, and to safe and peaceful neighborhoods—all these and more are closely linked to the future of our schools, to the ability of communities to educate their children. Nowhere is this interdependence more nakedly apparent than in New Orleans, where the infrastructure was blown away to lay bare the underpinnings of neglect and abandonment by the powerful forces who could have made a difference.

The real—not manufactured—crisis we confront is one not only of schools but of cities. Its resolution will not emanate Oz-like from the chambers of the city fathers, the magnanimous leaders of foundations, banks, and governments. If the school community is excluded from the change process, doesn't share the vision, or is just plain not ready for the change, it isn't going to happen. All the foundation money in the world will not make it happen. Neither will privatization schemes, federal mandates, or the threat of sanctions on low-performing schools.

Public schools and school systems, though quite capable of reform, usually require an outside catalyst or critical force within the community to set the spark, push change, and deepen it. The question is, what is that force in an arena of contending interests? For example, can any reform be successful without corporate and foundation actors? And if not, how can we keep the reform effort true to its democratic roots? Finally, how can democratic experiments and innovative practices such as the small-schools movement keep from losing their core values as they face the power of the Ownership Society?

The early small-schools movement, inspired by small schools in East Harlem and teacher-led experiments in Philadelphia and Chicago, provided just such a catalytic force. It offered teachers and parents in particular a handle—a way forward in trying to break out of those "regularities" by engaging teachers and whole school communities in a radical and comprehensive transformation process. The community, especially parents, supported the reforms fortified by a high degree of organization and articulate and creative leadership and in desperate need for better schools for its children. However, as the education reform movement grew and began to show its dynamic potential, it collided head-on with the might of an administration and conservative business interests, both with an ideological commitment toward maintaining privilege, promoting privatization, and hanging on to control. That collision knocked the small school and charter school movement off its track and derailed school reform, at least for the time being.

Though the small-schools movement owes a lot to its forerunners, from the progressive independent schools of the Eight-Year study to the Freedom Schools and the alternative democratic schools of the 1960s, the movement now needs to go well beyond those experiments to propel change in a traditional, hidebound system of public schools. Creating smaller learning environments wherein students are highly visible and known well by teachers, and where those teachers work in communities of professionals can no longer be viewed as an experiment. As we have shown in previous chapters, there is abundant evidence to demonstrate the effectiveness of such environments, especially when compared to the large factory model. The only dispute is over change strategies. How do we get there from here?

The small-schools movement must offer a different narrative from the one being projected by the powerful network of right-wing think tanks, another way of looking at the big picture of public education, and a set of politics other than the disaster politics presented in the usual commission reports. The early small-schools movement represented a strong counter-narrative, one that could generate community engagement and creative, collaborative problem solving. This narrative combines badly needed technological and organizational innovation with the ongoing historic struggle for civil rights, social justice, and educational equity. This narrative is mindful of its roots in the fight to educate and achieve full equality for the descendants of slaves and newly arrived immigrants. The process is less about efficiencies and more about problem solving. It deeply prizes participation and the notion that the people with the problems are also the people with solutions.

How are these guiding principles reflected in the change process in schools? The design for change includes lots of supports for teachers and plenty of time for teacher planning, peer coaching, and reflective dialogue. When planning for school reform or restructuring, the starting point must be consideration of each school's unique conditions. Though replicable models can be useful, they are often forced into inappropriate settings, such as kidney or heart transplants with incompatible donors or patients. All too often, top-down, model-driven reforms ignore the particular conditions at each school, its different traditions, demographics, previous experience (both positive and negative) with these same or other reform initiatives. Some schools may need more or less time than others to implement a given reform strategy despite the time line arbitrarily set by supporting foundations. So much depends on factors such as the level of preexisting support or buy-in from the teachers and the rest of the school community; the experience of the school's principal and his or her skills leading systemic change; the condition of the school facility; or capacity and quality of external supports, university or business partners.

Using a force-field analysis, taking an assets inventory, or doing a feasibility study are good starting points. The field usually has three columns and includes positive forces for change (+), middle forces (+ −), and forces of resistance (−). Data should include interviews and conversations with faculty, administration, and staff members; focus-group discussions with students and parents; and reviews of available test score information, dropout rates, existing programs, and the like. The purpose isn't to label anything or anyone as a "negative force" or to see any factor in a static or linear way. Rather, it's to view the change process as dynamic and multi-dimensional. The force-field idea is borrowed from social-psychologist Kurt Lewin's approach to dealing with group conflict, learning, and adolescence, in a repressive society.[3] When we look at the field of change in this way, taking into account staff attitudes, available resources, and experience with existing programs, we often find building blocks and things that are already working well. These positive forces are often things that systemic change models overlook as most of these models take public school failure for granted.

We usually find, for example, that if school leaders try to change too many things at once, such as revamping the curriculum, restrucuring into small learning communities, bringing in new assessments, changing the school leadership, they push the forces in the middle, those willing but somewhat skeptical about reform, over into the negative column three. On the other hand, if new restructuring initiatives result only in endless planning meetings and nothing ever really changes, demoralization sets in, and column one begins to disintegrate. This approach requires artful and skilled school leaders, principals, or lead teachers who are grounded in school realities and who don't run too far ahead of or behind their troops (sorry about the military metaphor, but on the other hand...). Skilled school leaders, fully prepared to lead in the creation of new schools or in the restructuring of large traditional schools, are hard to come by. Most of the university-based leadership programs we have seen or been part of do little to prepare principals for the task at hand. Alternative certification programs for school leaders are often singularly focused on new start-up schools or charters and provide few of the skills needed to lead a comprehensive, school-wide or system-wide change initiative. Without such a leadership program in place at the start, top-down reform initiative, such as Chicago's Renaissance 2010 plan to create 100 new schools in a decade, Mayor Bloomberg's race to start hundreds of new schools in New York, or the plan for privately managed charters schools in New Orleans, are severely hindered from the start.

On the basis of a careful assessment of the field, including the capacity of school leadership, rather than on the demands and timelines of the funders or the bureaucrats, the change process can get off on a good foot. This kind of approach also engenders a sense of democratic ownership over the change process, allows leaders to use their skills, and avoids the type of problems we found at Denver's Manual High School (described in Chapter 4) and other failed top-down, grant-driven attempts at restructuring.

When Sarason wrote about "the predictable failure of school reform," he offered a critique of "tinkering" around the edges of reform. Public schools then were in deep trouble but in a way different from that of today. Progressive educators at that time were in the forefront of a movement that often involved curriculum reform. A few radicals at the time were also considering the structure, culture, and organization of traditional schools.

Today, public schools are fighting for their very survival in the face of powerful forces that would seemingly like to do away with all public space. Parent organizations and teachers' unions are threatened. Questions of assessment and accountability have been pushed up to the top of the list because they drive so much of what teachers do in the classroom.

In New Jersey, for example, the state with the highest high school graduation rates in the country, parents and educators are fighting a defensive battle to retain a multiple-assessment approach to testing their kids, an approach that transcends standardized testing and includes performance assessments, as a way of ensuring that all students can demonstrate what they know and are able to do. Through the use of projects, for example, teaching can be geared more toward student interests rather than toward the standardized tests. There are several groups that have been organized to support teachers efforts in developing authentic, non-standardized assessments. Organizations such as FairTest have a wealth of experience backed by credible research in areas of testing and assessment.

On the policy front, groups such as the Forum on Education and Democracy, formed by a notable list of educators and scholars, including George Wood, Deborah Meier, Linda Darling-Hammond, Pedro Noguera, Ted Sizer, Gloria Ladson-Billings, and others, have played an important role in pushing for radical changes in the No Child Left Behind (NCLB) Act. After eight years in power and control of Congress, the wheels appear to be coming off many Ownership Society programs and policies, including reauthorization of the NCLB. Reauthorization has run into a wall and isn't likely to happen without fundamental changes in its approach to funding and the elimination of many of its most damaging and punitive assessment policies. Even a significant group of the NCLB's conservative supporters have jumped ship.

Programs such as Reading First, which may have had some sparkle just a few years ago, are now beginning to lose that luster. School voucher programs, though still very much alive, have been forced onto the back burner. Vouchers are now more a political wedge issue than a viable privatization initiative. The current network of cronyism around the Department of Education has been exposed in the Reading First, media bribery, and student loan scandals.

Heavily politicized and top-down reform strategies, run out of mayors' offices in districts such as New York and Chicago, are facing strong opposition after showing less than stellar results. School communities want reform done *with* them, not *to* them. Research continues to show the unspectacular performance of the EMOs and for-profit charter schools.

Despite several attempts by Republicans to defund the Smaller Learning Community funding initiatives from the K–12 education budget, these effective programs for high school restructuring, which began under the Clinton administration as a response to the school shootings at Columbine High, still manage to survive. The same holds true for school-to-career funding under the Perkins grant.

Community pushback against for-profit education management organizations (EMOs) such as Edison Schools has closed down their operations in some cities and has led to intense scrutiny and stronger accountability measures in others. That high level of accountability is vital if charters are going to continue as real public schools. However, accountability does not mean sameness.

We need good, not just more, small and charter schools. School boards need to see them as a limited but critical part of the public school system and support them as centers for innovation and experimentation, which spread best practices to the rest of the system.

Teachers' unions need to see small and charter schools as new areas of membership and make adjustments to the way they view contracts. There is no reason why union-board contracts have to be so large and all encompassing that they can't accommodate unique conditions in smaller or alternative schools, especially when the teachers in those schools agree to wave or modify certain work rules. Such arrangements and compromises have already been made in urban districts such as Boston, with its Pilot Schools, and Los Angeles, with the Green Dot Charters.

Charter school authorizers need strong accountability measures and can't simply be cheerleaders for charters as a group. Small schools and charters don't need any more cheerleaders, especially now that so many are being run by for-profit companies. They are not the experimental underdogs they were in their early days.

The current drive to restore teachers' collective bargaining rights and new teacher-union organizing drives should help to keep things honest and the playing field even. Some charter school operators such as Green Dot are finding that it's possible and even advantageous to have collective bargaining rights for teachers and to treat teachers as professionals rather than line workers. New York United Federation of Teachers (UFT) president Randi Weingarten recently responded in the spirit of Albert Shanker by extending an open hand to Green Dot, opening up new possibilities for tactical alliances where a year ago there were none. Similar meetings between the unions and Green Dot are taking place in Chicago. At a recent panel discussion we held in Chicago, Green Dot founder Steve Barr, Chicago Teachers Union President Marilyn Stewart, and Illinois Education Association (IEA) Director Jo Anderson all found common ground on the need for a partnership between unions and charter schools.

We would take the concept even farther. Parent and community-based organizations also have major roles to play in the new school reform coalitions and in the creation and development of small and charter schools. That could mean the creation of parent unions, such as the 10,000-member union that

Barr helped to organize. In Chicago, it could mean a restoration of the elected local school councils such as those embodied in the 1988 School Reform Act. Some charter operators worry that having teacher unions and strong parent councils will impede their autonomy, and to some degree it may. However, the trade-off is the power that these groups bring and the commitment and sense of teacher and community ownership needed for long-term success.

In the predominantly Mexican immigrant community of Little Village, on Chicago's south side, a two-year battle for a new high school culminated in a nineteen-day hunger strike by parents that led to creation of Little Village High School. The school is now the pride of Chicago's school system. It is a campus made up of four small schools, each with its own faculty, student cohort, curricular focus, and high degree of autonomy.

In Oakland, California, the public schools were so crowded that elementary schools had to cannibalize their playgrounds with portable classroom structures to hold the ever-increasing overflow of children. Parents and teachers of the district's 54,000 students were gravely concerned about the safety and effectiveness of the schools and frustrated by the combination of bureaucratic intransigence and chronic financial crisis, which sandbagged every creative proposal.

Beginning in 1999, the Oakland Community Organization (OCO), a large, parish-based parent group, began mobilizing adults to investigate possible solutions and to take political action in pursuit of them. OCO joined forces with a coalition of community and parent groups and with the Bay Area Coalition of Equitable Schools, which was deeply involved in organizing groups of teachers on the same issues.

Before these struggles for public school improvement took place, each community had been largely defined by its deficits, pathologies, and lack of resources. In each case, through organization and visionary leadership, ordinary people—

parents, neighbors, students, and teachers—were able to do extraordinary things, leverage resources, and impact policy decisions to improve public schooling. For us, these two communities have set a high standard for civic engagement in school reform.

Civic engagement holds the key to both saving and improving public education and rebuilding cities and communities trying to rebound from deindustrialization and the accompanying urban blight, fragmentation, isolation, and under-funding of public education. It's precisely the capacity for civic engagement that has been stifled and subverted by the top-down business-reform strategies prevalent under the Ownership Society. Though these strategies may lead to some short-term gains, perceived or real, they mainly tend to replicate the system's inequalities, reinforce segregation, and push more and more poor and minority students out of school. This is not to say that public–private partnerships are not necessary or at times don't play a key or decisive role in successful campaigns. However, all too often, especially under current models of privatization and erosion of public space, those partnerships haven't been real, and the public part has been undermined or removed completely.

One example of such a faux partnership was the Gates-funded initiative to redesign Denver's Manual High School into three small schools that began in 2001 and ended five years later in failure. The initiative failed largely owing to the lack of community engagement. The result was an initial retreat back to the comprehensive high school model and ultimately the closing of Manual, leaving in its wake community anger and demoralization.

Another example is Chicago's Renaissance 2010 plan to create 100 new small schools over a ten-year period. The program was drafted by the Civic Committee of the Commercial Club of Chicago with the mayor's imprimatur and carried out in cahoots with the city's biggest foundations and universities. The only thing missing was the very thing that could have made Renaissance 2010 a success—an engaged school community working in coalition with the CPS leadership and the business community. However, as the plan morphed into a school-closing and union-busting initiative, it lost community support and reversed all the important progress made in the first decade of Chicago's fabled school reform movement.

The Bloomberg-Klein reforms in New York, again backed by heavy private investment, opened the door to widespread privatization of public school management and support programs along with massive school closings or, as the *Village Voice* put it: "what for [Deborah] Meier was an innovation has become, for Klein and Bloomberg, a bulldozer." The mayor's new small schools and charters have so far failed to produce better learning outcomes, even though they have been heavily funded and even though there has been widespread discrimination, particularly against English-language learners and kids with disabilities in new school recruitment. When parent groups rallied in protest of the mayor's plan, he appointed a "chief parent engagement officer" to coopt the growing grass-roots movement.

Veteran Chicago community organizer Madeline Talbott, the director of the Association of Community Organizations for Reform Now (ACORN), sees a natural link between community engagement and small schools.

> "In the early days, small schools valued community and didn't view communities as external," Talbott told us in a recent interview. "Many poor folks understood the value of small schools and had even gone to small schools in their previous country or in the South. Our members don't instinctively oppose charters but don't like limitations on right to organize. It's a shame charters were tied to union busting. Why prohibit it? School reform captured by a radical ideological bunch. They shouldn't be allowed to develop their own private interests apart

those from those of traditional public schools. After all, they are public schools.

Talbott was most critical of those who would "bypass the community" or who think they know what's best for the people and "involve them just enough."[5] ACORN was among the many Chicago community-based organizations that opposed the Renaissance 2010 and Mid-South plans to arbitrarily close dozens of schools while turning others over to EMOs. For this, Talbott said, ACORN paid a heavy price:

> We supported efforts to beat the Mid-South plan. It was dead on arrival. They never talked about it again. But the foundation community really took it personally. Several foundations, including the Steans Family Fund, cut us off. They would do better to reach out to the community. We rely on the dues money from our members, so we do fine. Groups that were supporting notion of top-down decided that we couldn't make it work that way. They were wrong.

ACORN is currently leading an effort to "grow your own teachers" in communities wherein the lack of qualified teachers has been the main problem facing local schools. She left us with three recommendations for school reformers:

- Don't be afraid to ask the people who have the greatest stake in reform.
- Provide the real data about what's going on, not just test scores; what kids are going through; access to quality preschool compared to what's going on in other schools.
- Look at teacher quality and turnover and grow your own.

Power philanthropists such as Gates and Broad have had to reconsider many of their own reform plans after their own top-down restructuring debacles such as the one at Manual High

School in Denver. Shake-ups at the top of the Gates Foundation may signal a new, more grounded approach to school reform philanthropy. We have learned the hard way, as have many others, that the change process is complex and often unpredictable. The very things we prepare for are often not the ones we end up confronting. That's one reason we are so critical of the surety of top-down reformers and their "scientifically proven" easily replicable approaches to change. Though all public schools share common problems, each school and each district is unique and has its own experiences, positive and negative, with reform; its own culture and traditions; its own demographics and community economic life; its own resource base and leadership capacity. Keeping the "public" in public education, resisting standardization and anonymity in schools, and demanding equity in resources and opportunity must remain a central part of reform. The enemies of democratic schooling are formidable and continue to have the upper hand. However, when you look at them from another perspective, they have lots of weaknesses, and we have lots going for us.

NOTES

NOTES TO THE INTRODUCTION

1. William Ayers and Michael Klonsky, "Renaissance 2010: The Small Schools Movement Meets the Ownership Society." *Phi Delta Kappan*, February 2006, pp. 453–7.
2. Arne Duncan, "Chicago's Renaissance 2010: Building Reform in the Age of Accountability." *Phi Delta Kappan*, February 2006, pp. 457–8.
3. Lewis Cohen, "It's Not About Management..." *Phi Delta Kappan*, February 2006, pp. 459–61.
4. Quoted at Snopes.com, <http://www.snopes.com/politics/quotes/ike.asp>.
5. William Ayers and Michael Klonsky, "Private Management of Chicago Schools is a Long Way from Mecca." *Phi Delta Kappan*, February 2006, pp. 461–3.
6. Dorothy Shipps, *School Reform, Corporate Style: Chicago, 1880–2000*. (Lawrence, KS: University of Kansas Press, 2006) p. 1.
7. Liz Duffrin, "National Funders Spur Grassroots Reform." *Catalyst*, March 2007.

NOTES TO CHAPTER 1

1. Ravi Dykema, "How Schools Fail Kids and How They Could Be Better: An Interview with Ted Sizer, retired founder of the Coalition of Essential Schools (CES)." *Nexus* (May/June 2002), http://www.nexuspub.com/articles/2002/may2002/interview1.htm (accessed July 26, 2007).

2. See Ted Sizer's trilogy of *Horace* books, *Horace's Hope: What Works for the American High School* (New York: Houghton Mifflin, 1997); *Horace's School: Redesigning the American High School* (New York: Houghton Mifflin, 1992); and *Horace's Compromise: The Dilemma of the American High School* (New York: Houghton Mifflin, 1984).

3. Sonja Steptoe and Claudia Wallis. "How to Bring Our Schools Out of the 20th Century." *Time*, December 10, 2006.

4. Joel I. Klein, "Changing the Culture of Urban Public Education." *Harvard Law & Policy Review*, Vol.1, No.1, April, 2007. http://www.hlpronline.com/2007/04/klein_01.html (accessed July 31, 2007).

5. National Center on Education and the Economy, *Tough Choices or Tough Times: The Report of the New Commission on the Skills of the American Workforce* (San Francisco, CA: Jossey-Bass, 2006).

6. Seymour Fliegel, *Miracle in East Harlem: The Fight for Choice in Public Education* (New York: Times Books, 1993).

7. Charles Payne, "More Than a Symbol of Freedom: Education for Liberation and Democracy." *Phi Delta Kappan*, September, 2003, pp. 22–8.

8. Charles Cobb, "Organizing the Freedom Schools." In *Freedom is a Constant Struggle: An Anthology of the Mississippi Civil Rights Movement*, ed. Susan Erenrich (Washington, DC: Cultural Center for Social Change, 1999).

9. Pat Ford and Michael Klonsky, "One Urban Solution: Small Schools." *Educational Leadership*, May 1994.

10. Michelle Fine, Michael Katz and Elaine Simon, "Poking Around: Outsiders View Chicago School Reform." *TC Record*, Vol. 99 No. 1, 1997.

11. Patricia Wasley, Linda C. Powell, Esther Mosak, Sherry P. King, Nicole E. Holland, Matt Gladden and Michelle Fine, *Small Schools: Great Strides – A Study of New Small Schools in Chicago* (New York: Bank Street College of Education, 2002).

12. Designs for Change. *The Big Picture: School-Initiated Reforms, Centrally Initiated Reforms, and Elementary School Achievement in Chicago (1990 to 2005)*. (Chicago, IL: Designs for Change, 2006).

, *The Big Picture: School-Initiated Reforms, Centrally Initiated Reforms, and Elementary School Achievement in Chicago (1990 to 2005)* (Chicago: Designs for Change, 2006).

13. Hillary Rodham Clinton, "Elementary and Secondary Education," http://clinton.senate.gov/issues/education/index.cfm?topic=elementary (accessed June 14, 2007).

14. Nancy Zuckerbrod, "2300 Schools: No Child Overhaul." *Time*, January 20, 2007.

15. "Can D.C. schools be fixed?" editorial, *Washington Post*, June 10, 2007.

16. Dorothy Shipps, *School Reform, Corporate Style: Chicago, 1880–2000* (Lawrence: University of Kansas, 2006), p. 17.

17. Civic Committee of the Commercial Club of Chicago *Left Behind: A Report of the Education Committee* (Chicago: Civic Committee of the Commercial Club of Chicago, 2003), http://www.commercialclubchicago.org/civiccommittee/initiatives/education/LEFT_BEHIND.pdf (accessed August 1, 2007).

18. Civic Committee of the Commercial Club of Chicago, p. 2

19. Janet Smith and David Stovall, "Urban Geographies, Racial Inequalities, and Policymaking: World Cities as Contexts for Black Education." Paper delivered at American Educational Research Association Conference, Chicago, 2007.

20. Veronica Anderson, "Smaller is Better." *Catalyst Chicago*, May 1998, http://www.catalyst-chicago.org/arch/05-98/058wmm01.htm (accessed August 1, 2007).

NOTES TO CHAPTER 2

1. "School Effort Boosts Business Test Publishers, Tutors And Teacher Trainers Realize Benefits." *Wall Street Journal*, December 24, 2004.

2. See David Berliner and Bruce Biddle, *The Manufactured Crisis: Myths, Fraud and the Attack on America's Public Schools* (Reading, MA: Addison-Wesley, 1995).

3. Kenneth Saltman, *Schooling and the Politics of Disaster* (New York: Routledge, 2007).

4. Fine, Interview July 20, 2007

5. Remarks at the No Child Left Behind Summit (April 27, 2006).

6. See Williamson M. Evers and Tom G. Palmer. "Constitutional Crossroads Rights and Wrongs." *National Review*, August 15, 2005, http://www.nationalreview.com/comment/evers_palmer200508150819.asp (accessed June 6, 2007).

7. Laura S. Hamilton, *et al.*, *Standards-based Accountability Under No Child Left Behind: Experiences of Teachers and Administrators in Three States* (Santa Monica, CA: Rand Corporation, 2007).

8. Tom Hayden and Dick Flacks, "The Port Huron Statement at Age 40." *The Nation*, August 2002, http://www.thenation.com/doc/20020805/hayden (accessed July 2, 2007).

9. See Newt Gingrich, "We must expand our investment in science." Testimony before the Senate Committee on Commerce, Science, and Transportation, http://commerce.senate.gov/hearings/052202 gingrich.pdf.

10. James B. Conant, *The American High School Today* (New York: McGraw-Hill, 1959).

11. Lawrence A. Cremin, *The Transformation of the School: Progressivism in American Education, 1876– 1957* (New York: Vintage Books, 1961).

12. National Commission of Excellence in Education, *A Nation at Risk: The Imperative for Educational Reform* (Washington, DC: U.S. Government Printing Office, 1983).

13. National Center on Education and the Economy, *Tough choices or Tough Times: The Report of the New Commission on the Skills of the American Workforce* (San Francisco, CA: Jossey-Bass, 2006).

14. Bill Moyers, "For America's Sake." *The Nation*, January 2007. http://www.thenation.com/doc/20070122/moyers (accessed July 2, 2007).

15. David Nakumura, "Big-name Consultants Greeted with Wariness." *Washington Post*, June 24, 2007; p. C06.

16. Herbert J. Walbert and Joseph Bast, *Education and Capitalism: How Overcoming Our Fear of Markets and Economics Can Improve America's Schools* (Palo Alto, CA: Hoover Institution Press, 2003), p. 83.

17. Stephen Moore, *Bullish on Bush: How George W. Bush's Ownership Society Will Make America Stronger* (New York: Derrydale, 2004).

18. "Wisconsin Lawmakers Express Mixed Reactions to State of Union." AP Wire, January 24, 2006, the Northwestern.com. http://www.thenorthwestern.com/apps/pbcs.dll/article?AID=/20070124/OSH/301240035.

19. Daniel Shulman, "Highway Privatization: 'This is All about Money.'" *Mother Jones*, February 13, 2007. http://www.motherjones.com/washington_dispatch/2007/02/defazio_house_committee_highway_privatization.html (accessed March 2, 2007).

20. Stephen Metcalf, "Reading Between the Lines." *The Nation*. January 28, 2002. http://www.thenation.com/doc/20020128/metcalf (accessed July 2, 2007).

21. James Harris, "Jeremy Scahill on Soldiers of Fortune." *Truthdig*, March 30, 2007. http://www.truthdig.com/interview/print/20070330_jeremy_scahill_on_soldiers_of_fortune/ (accessed July 30, 2007).

22. Rod Paige, *The War against Hope: How Teachers' Unions Hurt Children, Hinder Teachers, and Endanger Public Education* (Nashville, TN: Thomas Nelson, 2006).

23. Paige, p. 190.

24. Terence Jeffrey, "Apply 'Ownership Society' Government Schools." Townhall.com, January 19, 2005. http://www.townhall.com/columnists/column.aspx?UrlTitle=apply_ownership_society_to_government_schools&ns=TerenceJeffrey&dt=01/19/2005&page=full&comments=true (accessed July 30, 2007).

25. Brendan Murray, "Bush's 'Ownership Society' Founders as U.S. Economy Weakens." Bloomberg.com, March 21, 2007. http://taxes.blogsome.com/2007/04/16/bushs-ownership-society-founders-as-us-economy-weakens/trackback/ (accessed July 30, 2007).

26. Robert B. Reich, "What Ownership Society?" TomPaine.common sense. September 2, 2004. http://www.tompaine.com/articles/what_ownership_society.php (accessed July 30, 2007).

27. "School Choice and the Ownership Society." Cato Institute, 2003. https://www.cato.org/special/ownership_society/school-ownership.html#1 (accessed June 2, 2007).

28. Paul Glastris, "Bush's Ownership Society: Why No One's Buying." *Washington Monthly*, Vol. 37, No. 12, December 2005.

29. Peter Drucker, *Managing in the Next Society* (New York: St. Martins Griffin, 2003), p. 29.

30. Ryan Sager, "The Ownership Society and its Discontents." *Reason*, Vol. 38, No.6 (2006), pp. 42–50 N.

31. Alex Molnar, David R. Garcia, Gary Miron, and Shannon Berry, *Profiles of For-Profit Education Management Organizations: 2005–2006* (Tempe, AZ: Commercialism in Education Research Unit, Arizona State University, 2005).

32. Patricia Burch, "The New Educational Privatization: Educational Contracting and High Stakes accountability." *Teachers College Record*, Vol. 108, No. 12 (New York: Columbia University, 2006).

33. Kay Stewart, "Obama: Vote Offers Choice." *Louisville Courier-Journal*, September 15, 2006.

34. Jean Schulte Scott, "Eye on Washington." *Healthcare Financial Management*, May 1, 2005.

35. Evan Cornog, "Let's Blame The Reader." *Columbia Journalism Review*, January 2005. http://www.cjr.org/issues/2005/1/cornog-readers.asp (accessed July 30, 2007).

36. Larry Cuban, "Making Public Schools Business-Like...Again." *PS: Political Science & Politics*, April, 2004. https://www.apsanet.org/imgtest/MakingPublicSchoolsBusinessLike.pdf (accessed July 31 2007).

37. Dan Lips, "Reagan's ABCs." *National Review*, March 22, 2001. http://www.nationalreview.com/comment/comment-lipsprint052201.html (accessed July 30, 2007).

38. John Hechinger and Anne Marie Chaker, "Did Revolving Door Lead To Student Loan Mess? Critics Blame Lax Oversight Resulting From Close Ties Of Industry, Government." *Wall Street Journal*, April 13, 2007; p. B1.

39. Kathleen Kennedy Manzo, "Reading Probe Will Continue on Capitol Hill." *Education Week*, Vol. 26, No. 31, April 4, 2007, pp. 1, 17.

40. Sam Dillon, "Report Says Education Officials Violated Rules in Awarding Initiative Grants." *New York Times*, September 23, 2006. http://select.nytimes.com/search/restricted/article?res=F60913FD35550C708EDDA00894DE404482#.

41. Chester Finn, "Table of treats." *Gadfly*, Vol. 7, No. 18, May 10, 2007. http://www.edexcellence.net/foundation/gadfly/issue.cfm?id=290 (accessed July 30, 2007).

42. "Inspector General Condemns Reading First Program." CREW press release, February 22, 2007. http://www.citizensforethics.org/press/newsrelease.php?view=204 (accessed July 30, 2007).

43. Kathleen Kennedy Manzo, "Ed. Dept. Allowed Singling Out Of 'Reading First' Products." *Education Week*, March 2, 2007, p. 13.

44. Holly Ramer, "Clinton Promises Education Improvements." *Boston Globe*, March 30, 2007. http://www.boston.com/news/education/k_12/articles/2007/03/30/clinton_criticizes_federal_funding_of_private_tutors/ (accessed July 30, 2007).

45. Deborah Meier, "Unintended Consequences." *Bridging Differences*, April 2, 2007. http://blogs.edweek.org/edweek/Bridging-Differences/2007/04/dear_diane_you_might_have.html.

NOTES TO CHAPTER 3

1. Winnie Hu, "Middle School Manages Distraction of Adolescents." *New York Times*, May 12, 2007. http://www.nytimes.com/2007/05/12/education/12middle.html?_r=1&ref=education&oref=slogin.

2. Michelle Fine "Not in our name." *Rethinking Schools*, Vol. 19, No. 4, July 1, 2005. http://www.rethinkingschools.org/archive/19_04/name 194.shtml.

3. Jeffrey Henig, Heath Brown, Natalie Lacireno-Paquet and Thomas T. Holyoke, *Charter Schools Can be Big and Bureaucratic, Too* (New York: Columbia University, Teachers College, 2005). http://www.newswise.com/articles/view/508979/.

4. P. Farber, "The Edison Project scores—and stumbles—in Boston." *Phi Delta Kappan*, Vol. 79, No. 7, November 1998, pp. 506–11.

5. Michelle Fine "Not in our name." Ibid.

6. "Exploding the Charter School Myth." editorial, *New York Times*, August 27, 2006. http://select.nytimes.com/search/restricted/article ?res=FB0D14FB3B5A0C748EDDA10894DE404482.

7. Samuel Freedman, "English Language Learners as Pawns in the School System's Overhaul." *New York Times*, May 10, 2007. http://www.nytimes.com/2007/05/09/education/09education.html.

8. Kim Sweet, *Small Schools, Few Choices: How New York City's High School Reform Effort Left Students with Disabilities Behind* (New York: Parents for Inclusive Education, Oct. 2006). http://www.nylpi.org/pub/High_School_Report.pdf.

9. Interview with Joe Nathan, May 11, 2007.

10. Christopher Whittle, *Crash Course* (New York: Riverhead, 2005).

11. Joe Nathan, *Charter Schools: Creating Hope and Opportunity for American Education* (San Francisco, CA: Jossey-Bass, 1966).

12. Ray Budde, *Education by Charter: Restructuring School Districts* (Portland, OR: NWRL, 1988).

13. Ray Budde and the origins of the "Charter Concept" by Ted Kolderie, June, 2005 in Education Evolving, http://www.educationevolving.org/pdf/Ray_Budde.pdf.

14. Ted Kolderie, "Chelsea Clinton and the D.C. schools." http://www.educationevolving.org/pdf/Chelsea_Clinton.pdf.

15. Chester E. Finn, Bruno V. Manno and Greg Vanourek, *Charter Schools In Action* (Princeton, NJ: Princeton University Press, 2000), p. 3.

16. Joe Nathan, *Charter Schools* (San Francisco, CA: Jossey-Bass, 1996), p. 63.

17. Michelle Fine, *Chartering Urban School Reform: Reflections on Public High Schools in the Midst of Change* (New York: Teachers College Press, 1994).

18. Chester E. Finn, Jr., Louann Bierlein, and Bruno V. Manno, *Charter Schools in Action: A First Look* (Washington, DC: Hudson Institute, 1996).

19. Finn, Manno, and Vanourek, op. cit.

20. Gerald Bracey, "The 11th Bracey Report on The Condition of Public Education." *Phi Delta Kappan*. online article http://www.pdkintl.org/kappan/k0110bra.htm.

21. Greg Richmond, "Piecing Together the Charter Puzzle." *Education Week*, Vol. 26, No. 33, 1997, pp. 28–9.

22. C. Furtwengler, "Policies and Privatization." *American School Board Journal*, Vol. 185, No. 4, 1998, p. 42.

23. Mallory Stark, "Lessons from Privately Managed Schools." Harvard Business School Online. http://hbswk.hbs.edu/archive/5189.html.

24. Elissa Gootman, "Schools Official Deflects Query About Stocks." *New York Times*, February 9, 2007, Section B, p. 1.

25. Whittle, p. 235.

26. Michael Scherer, "Some of Bush's Largest Donors Stand to Profit from Privatizing Public Education." March 5, 2001. http://www.motherjones.com/news/special_reports/mojo_400/schools.html.

27. Kent Fischer, "Public Schools Inc.," *St. Petersburg Times*, September 15, 2002.

28. Liza Featherstone, "On the Wal-Mart Money Trail." *The Nation*, November 21, 2005.

29. Jay Mathews, "Looking at KIPP, Coolly and Carefully," April 24, 2007, *Washington Post*. http://www.washingtonpost.com/wp-dyn/content/article/2007/04/24/AR2007042400558_pf.html.

30. Allison Sherry, "Cole Charter Set for Closure." *Denver Post*, September 11, 2006. http://www.denverpost.com/ci_4997813.

31. Teresa Taylor Williams, "Low Test scores Threaten Two Academies." *Muskegon Chronicle*, July 9, 2006.

32. Brian P. Gill, Ron Zimmer, Jolley Bruce Christman, and Suzanne Blanc, *State Takeover, School Restructuring, Private Management, Student Achievement in Philadelphia* (Santa Monica, CA: Rand Corp., 2007).

33. Paul Socolar, "Edison Gets $1.6 M for Students It Doesn't Have," *Philadelphia Public School Notebook*, Spring 2007 Edition. http://www.thenotebook.org/editions/2007/spring/edison.htm.

34. Gary Miron, "Evaluation of the Delaware Charter School Reform: Year 1 Report." December, 2004. The Evaluation Center, Western Michigan University.

35. Diane R. Stepp, "Charter School Companies Eyeing Georgia." *Atlanta Journal-Constitution*, April 24, 2007.

36. Sarah Schweitzer, "Proposed Charter School Debated." *St. Petersburg Times*, December 31, 2000. Online: http://www.sptimes.com/News/123100/TampaBay/Proposed_charter_scho.shtml.

37. Joel Rubin, "Locke High seeks to leave L.A. Unified." *Los Angeles Times*, May 10, 2007.

NOTES TO CHAPTER 4

1. Michelle Fine, phone interview by the author, July 22, 2007.
2. David Herszenhorn, "Patrons' Sway Leads to Friction in Charter School." *New York Times*, June 28, 2007, p. A1.
3. Jeffrey T. Fouts, Duane B. Baker, Carol J. Brown and Shirley C. Riley, *Leading the Conversion Process: Lessons Learned and Recommendations for Converting to Smaller Learning Communities* (Seattle, WA: Bill and Melinda Gates Foundation, 2006), p. 5.
4. Caroline Hendrie, "High Schools Nationwide Paring Down." *Education Week*, Vol. 23, Issue 40, June 16, 2004, pp. 1, 28–30.
5. Allison Sherry, "Manual's Slow Death." *Denver Post*, May 7, 2006.
6. Holly Yettick, "Separating for Success." *Rocky Mountain News*, December 9, 2002.
7. Smallschools Listserv, post 1858, September 5, 2002.
8. Seymour Sarason, *Revisiting "The Culture of the School and the Problem of Change"* (New York: Teachers College Press, 1996), p. 335.
9. Carol Kreck, "Manual High Tackles Disputes: Student Group Says School Segregated, Lacks Key Classes." *Denver Post*, August 9, 2002. http://groups.yahoo.com/group/smallschools/message/1814 (accessed July 31, 2007).
10. Jay Greene and William C. Symonds, "Bill Gates Gets Schooled." *Business Week*, June 26, 2006.
11. See Paris Achen's articles in the *Mail Tribune*: "Grant Awaits 'Small School': Educators Scramble To Meet April Deadline." March 8, 2007. http://www.mailtribune.com/archive/2007/0308/local/stories/ossi.htm (accessed July 31, 2007), and "North Medford Loses Schools Initiative Money" (accessed June 26, 2007).
12. Charles Piller, Edmund Sanders and Robyn Dixon, "Dark Cloud Over Good Works of Gates Foundation." *Los Angeles Times*, January 7, 2007. http://www.latimes.com/news/nationworld/nation/la-na-gatesx07jano7,0,4205044,full.story?coll=la-home-headlines (accessed July 31, 2007).
13. Michael Paulson, "Gingrich Drives Hard on Behalf of Microsoft." *Seattle Post-Intelligencer*, August 26, 1998.
14. Stephen Labaton, "Microsoft Finds Legal Defender in Justice Department." *New York Times*, June 10, 2007. http://www.nytimes.

com/2007/06/10/business/10microsoft.html?ex=1186027200&en=d 6a2435bf5accc88&ei=5070 (accessed July 31, 2007).

15. Benjamin Barber, "Is a Philanthropic Monopoly a Good Thing?" Marketplace, National Public Radio, June 30, 2006.

16. Rick Cohen, "Buffett Gift Raises Questions." *Philanthropy Journal*, letter to the editor, July 10, 2006.

17. Holly Yeager, "Concern Over Scrutiny of Do-it-All Philanthropists." *Financial Times*, July 5, 2006. http://www.ncrp.org/ar-07052006-financialtimes-concernoverscrutinyofdo-it-all-philanthropists.asp (accessed July 31, 2007).

18. Joe Allen, "The Horrible House of Walton: Lying, Cheating and Swindling Their Way To The Top." December 2, 2005. http://www. ncrp.org/ar-120205-socialistworker-horriblehouse.asp (accessed July 31, 2007).

19. Bryan C. Hassel and Thomas Toch, "Big Box: How the Heirs of the Wal-Mart Fortune Have Fueled the Charter School Movement." *Education Sector*, November 7, 2006. http://www.educationsector.org/analysis/ analysis_show.htm?doc_id=422193 (accessed July 31, 2007).

20. Eric W. Robelen, "Venture Fund Fueling Push for New Schools." *Education Week*, Vol. 20, No. 39, January 17, 2007, pp. 25–9.

21. Michael Barbaro and Stephanie Strom, "Wal-Mart Finds an Ally in Conservatives." *New York Times*, September 8, 2006.

22. Elise Young, "N.J. School Voucher Fight Tilts to the Right." *The Record*, July 24, 2006, in NCRP website. http://www.ncrp.org/AR-072406-TheRecord-NJSchoolVoucherFightTiltstotheRight.doc.asp.

23. Ibid.

24. *The American Heritage Dictionary* (New York: Houghton-Miflin, 2000).

NOTES TO CHAPTER 5

1. John Saloma, *Ominous Politics: The New Conservative Labyrinth* (New York: Hill & Wang, 1984).

2. Mary Jacoby, "Madame Cheney's Cultural Revolution." Salon.com, August 26, 2004. http://dir.salon.com/story/news/feature/2004/ 08/26/lynne_cheney/index.html (accessed August 1, 2007).

3. Saloma, *op. cit.*

4. Former FCC Chair Reed Hundt, cited in Pepi Leistyna "No Corporation Left Behind" in Kenneth J. Saltman (ed.) *Schooling and the Politics of Disaster* (New York: Routledge Press, 2007), p. 131.

5. William Baroody, Heritage Foundation's *Policy Review*, quoted in "Media & Communications Efforts: From a report by NCRP." MediaTransparency.org   http://www.mediatransparency.org/ conservativephilanthropypageprinterfriendly.php?conservativePhilant hropyPageID=12.

6. "Media and Communications Efforts. From a report by NCRP." MediaTransparency.org   http://www.mediatransparency.org/ conservativephilanthropypageprinterfriendly.php?conservative PhilanthropyPageID=12 (accessed August 1, 2007).

7. Seymour Fleigel and J. Macguire, *Miracle in East Harlem: The Fight for Choice in Public Education* (New York: Three Rivers Press, 1994).

8. Richard Hernnstein and Charles Murray, *The Bell Curve* (New York: Free Press, 1994).

9. Quoted in *Buying a Movement: Right-Wing Foundations and American Politics* (Washington, DC: People For The American Way).

10. Paul Krugman, "Don't Blame Bush." *New York Times*, May 18, 2007.

11. Chester Finn, "Jonathan Kozol Launches Anti-NCLB Network." *Education Gadfly*, Vol. 6, No. 26, June 29, 2006.

12. Chester Finn and Mike Petrilli, "Fool Me Twice: No Child Left Behind Again. Only Worse." *National Review*, February 2006. http://article. nationalreview.co=ODRhNGQoNzJkNjc3OGQyOWViZGJjZmIoNzY4 ZDhjMzk=(accessed August 1, 2007).

13. Chester Finn, "Peer Review." *The Education Gadfly*, May 10, 2007. http://www.edexcellence.net/foundation/gadfly/issue.cfm?id=290 August 1, 2007.

14. Chester Finn, "Charter Schools in Action: Renewing Public Education." Speech at the Askwith Education Form, *HGSE News*, February 2000. http://www.gse.harvard.edu/news/features/forums_finn.html.

15. Petrilli, Michael. "Why Not Catholic Charter Schools?" *The Education Gadfly*, December 6, 2007. http://www.edexcellence.net/foundation/ gadfly/index.cfm#3732.

NOTES TO CHAPTER 6

1. Michael Klonsky, "Small Schools And Teacher Professional Development." *Eric Digest* (Charleston, WV: ERIC Clearinghouse On Rural Education And Small Schools, AEL, 2002).

2. Nancy Mohr, "Small Schools Are Not Miniature Large Schools. Potential Pitfalls and Implications for Leadership," in W. Ayers, M. Klonsky and G. Lyon (eds) *A Simple Justice: The Challenge of Small Schools* (New York: Teachers College Press, 2000), pp. 139–58.

3. Paulo Freire and Myles Horton, *We Make the Road by Walking: Conversations on Education and Social Change* (Philadelphia, PA: Temple University Press, 1990).

4. Seymour Sarason, *Revisiting "The Culture of the School and the Problem of Change"* (New York: Teachers College Press, 1996).

5. Madeline Talbott, phone interview with author, July 18, 2007.

BIBLIOGRAPHY

Anderson, Veronica. "Smaller is Better." *Catalyst Chicago*. May 1998.

Applegate, Brooks, and Gary Miron. "Teacher Attrition In Charter Schools." *Education Policy Reseach Unit*. May 23, 2007.

Ayers, William and Michael Klonsky. "Navigating a Restless Sea: The Continuing Struggle to Achieve a Decent Education for African American Youngsters in Chicago," *Journal of Negro Education* 63 (1994) 5–18.

Ayers, William and Michael Klonsky. "Private Management of Chicago Schools Is a Long Way From Mecca." *Phi Delta Kappan*. February 2006. 461–3.

Ayers, William and Michael Klonsky. "Renaissance 2010: The Small Schools Movement Meets The Ownership Society." *Phi Delta Kappan*. February 2006. 453–7.

Barbaro, Michael and Stephanie Strom. "Wal-Mart Finds an Ally in Conservatives." *New York Times*. September 8, 2006.

Bast, Joseph and Herbert J. Walberg. *Education and Capitalism: How Overcoming Our Fear of Markets and Economics Can Improve America's Schools*. (Palo Alto, CA: Hoover Institution Press, 2003).

Benton, Joshua, and Holly Hacker. "Cheating's Off the Charts at Charter Schools." *Dallas Morning News* June 4, 2007.

Berliner, David C. and Bruce J. Biddle. *The Manufactured Crisis: Myths, Fraud, and the Attack on America's Public Schools*. (Reading, MA: Addison-Wesley, 1995).

Bosman, Julie. "Public Schools Feed Multitudes This Summer." *New York Times.* July 10, 2007.

Bracey, Gerald. "The 11th Bracey Report on the Condition of Public Education." *Phi Delta Kappan.* October 21, 2001, 83: 157–69.

Bracey, Gerald. "The AFT Charter School Study: Not News." Education Policy Studies Laboratory, Arizona State University. August 20, 2004. http://epsl. asu.edu/epru/POV/EPSL-0408-121-EPRU-POV.pdf.

Budde, Ray. *Education by Charter: Restructuring School Districts, Key to Long Term Continuing Improvement in American Education.* (Portland, OR: Learning Innovations, 1988).

Burch, Patricia. "The New Educational Privatization: Educational Contracting and High Stakes Accountability." *Teachers College Record.* Vol. 108, No. 12. New York: Columbia University, 2006.

Casey, Leo. "Do Charter Schools Need Unions?" *Edwize.* June 28, 2006. http:// Edwize.Org/Do-Charter-Schools-Need-Unions.

Cato Institute. "School Choice and the Ownership Society," 2003 (June 2, 2007).

Christman, Jolley Bruce, and Amy Rhodes. *Civic Engagement and Urban School Improvement: Hard-To-Learn Lessons from Philadelphia.* (Philadelphia, PA: Consortium for Policy Research in Education, 2002).

Citizens for Responsibility and Ethics in Washington. "Inspector General Condemns Reading First Program," CREW press release, February 22, 2007. http://www.citizensforethics.org/press/newsrelease.php?view=204

Civic Committee of the Commercial Club of Chicago. *Left Behind: A Report of the Education Committee.* Chicago: Civic Committee of the Commercial Club of Chicago, 2003.

Cobb, Charles. "Organizing the Freedom Schools," in Susan Erenrich (ed.) *Freedom Is a Constant Struggle: An Anthology of the Mississippi Civil Rights Movement.* (Washington, DC: Cultural Center for Social Change, 1999).

Cohen, Lewis. "It's Not About Management…" *Phi Delta Kappan.* February 2006. 459–61.

Cohen, Rick. "Buffett Gift Raises Questions" [letter to the editor]. *Philanthropy Journal.* July 10, 2006.

Conant, James B. *The American High School Today.* (New York: McGraw-Hill, 1959).

Cornog, Evan. "Let's Blame the Reader." *Columbia Journalism Review.* January 2005.

Cremin, Lawrence A. *The Transformation of the School: Progressivism in American Education, 1876–1957.* (New York: Vintage Books, 1961).

Designs for Change. *The Big Picture: School-Initiated Reforms, Centrally Initiated Reforms, and Elementary School Achievement in Chicago (1990 to 2005)*. (Chicago, IL: Designs for Change, 2006).

Dillon, Sam. "Report Says Education Officials Violated Rules in Awarding Initiative Grants." *New York Times*. September 23, 2006.

Dillon, Sam. "Maverick Leads Charge for Charter Schools." *New York Times*. July 23, 2007.

Dixon, Robyn, Charles Piller, and Edmund Sanders. "Dark Cloud Over Good Works of Gates Foundation." *Los Angeles Times*. January 7, 2007.

Drucker, Peter. *Managing in the Next Society*. (New York: St. Martins Griffin, 2003).

Duffrin, Liz. "National Funders Spur Grassroots Reform." *Catalyst*. March 2007.

Duncan, Arne. "Chicago's Renaissance 2010: Building Reform in the Age of Accountability." *Phi Delta Kappan*. Feburary, 2006, 87(6): 457–8.

Dykema, Ravi. "How Schools Fail Kids and How They Could Be Better: An Interview with Ted Sizer, retired founder of the Coalition of Essential Schools (CES)." *Nexus*, (May/June 2002).

Farber, P. "The Edison Project Scores and Stumbles in Boston." *Phi Delta Kappan*. November 1, 1998, 79: 506–11.

Featherstone, Liza. "On the Wal-Mart Money Trail." *The Nation*. November 21, 2005.

Fine, Michelle. *Chartering Urban School Reform: Reflections on Public High Schools in the Midst of Change (Professional Development and Practice)*. (New York: Teachers College Press, 1994).

Fine, Michelle. "Not in Our Name." *Rethinking Schools*. July 1, 2005.

Fine, Michelle, Michael Katz and Elaine Simon. "Poking Around: Outsiders View Chicago School Reform." *Teachers College Record*. Vol. 99. No. 1. New York: Columbia University, 1997.

Finn, Chester E., Jr., Louann Bierlein and Bruno V. Manno. *Charter Schools in Action: A First Look*. (Washington, DC: Hudson Institute, 1996).

Finn, Chester and Mike Petrilli. "Fool Me Twice: No Child Left Behind Again. Only Worse." *National Review*. February 2006. August 1, 2007.

Finn, Chester E., Bruno V. Manno and Greg Vanourek. *Charter Schools in Action: Renewing Public Education*. (Princeton, NJ: Princeton University Press, 2000).

Fliegel, Seymour. *Miracle in East Harlem: The Fight for Choice in Public Education.* (New York: Times Books, 1993).

Freedman, Samuel. "English Language Learners as Pawns in the School System's Overhaul." *New York Times*. May 9, 2007. May 10, 2007.

Ford, Pat and Michael Klonsky. "One Urban Solution: Small Schools." *Educational Leadership*. May 1994.

Fouts, Jeffrey T., Duane B. Baker, Carol J. Brown and Shirley C. Riley. *Leading the Conversion Process: Lessons Learned and Recommendations for Converting to Smaller Learning Communities. (*Seattle: Bill & Melinda Gates Foundation, 2006).

Freire, Paolo and Myles Horton. *We Make the Road by Walking: Conversations on Education and Social Change*. (Philadelphia, PA: Temple University Press, 1990).

Furtwengler, C. "Policies and Privatization." *American School Board Journal*. Vol. 185, No. 4 (1998), p. 42.

Gingrich, Newt. "We Must Expand our Investment in Science." Testimony before the Senate Committee on Commerce, Science, and Transportation. August 1, 2007. http://commerce.senate.gov/hearings/052202gingrich.pdf

Glastris, Paul. "Bush's Ownership Society: Why No One's Buying." *Washington Monthly*. Vol. 37, No. 12 (December 2005).

Green, Elizabeth. "How New Generation of Reformers Targets Democrats on Education." *New York Sun*. May 31, 2007.

Greene, Jay and William C. Symonds. "Bill Gates Gets Schooled." *Business Week*. June 26, 2006.

Hamilton, Laura S., Abby Robyn, Brian M. Stecher, Jennifer Sloan McCombs, Julie A. Marsh. *Standards-Based Accountability under No Child Left Behind: Experiences of Teachers and Administrators in Three States*. (Santa Monica, CA: Rand Corporation, 2007).

Hassel, Bryan C. and Thomas Toch. "Big Box: How the Heirs of the Wal-Mart Fortune Have Fueled the Charter School Movement." *Education Sector*. November 7, 2006 (July 31, 2007).

Harris, James. "Jeremy Scahill on Soldiers of Fortune." *Truthdig*. March 20, 2007.

Hayden, Tom and Dick Flacks. "The Port Huron Statement at Age 40." *The Nation*. August 2002. July 2, 2007.

Hernnstein, Richard and Charles Murray, *The Bell Curve*. (New York: Free Press, 1994).

Herszenhorn, David. "Patrons' Sway Leads to Friction in Charter School." *New York Times*. June 28, 2007, p.A1.

Hu, Winnie. "Middle School Manages Distractions of Adolescence." *The New York Times*. May 12, 2007.

Jacoby, Mary. "Madame Cheney's Cultural Revolution." Salon.com. August 26, 2004.

Kahlenberg, Richard. *Tough Liberal: Albert Shanker and the Battles over Schools, Unions, Race, and Democracy.* (New York: Columbia University Press, 2007).

Kennedy, Mike. "The Reformers." *American School & University.* June 2007.

Klein, Joel. "Changing the Culture of Urban Public Education." *Harvard Law & Policy Review.* Vol. 1. No. 1 (April 2007).

Klein, Naomi. *The Shock Doctrine: The Rise of Disaster Capitalism* (New York: Henry Holt, 2007).

Klonsky, Michael. *Small Schools: The Numbers Tell a Story.* (Chicago, IL: University of Illinois at Chicago Small Schools Workshop, 1995).

Kolderie, Ted. "Charter Schools: The States Begin To Withdraw The 'Exclusive.'" *Network News and Views.* 4 (1994), pp. 103–8.

Kolderie, Ted. "Chelsea Clinton and the D.C. Schools." *Education Evolving.* January 1, 1993. (July 28, 2007). http://www.educationevolving.org/pdf/Chelsea_Clinton.pdf.

Kreck, Carol. "Manual High Tackles Disputes: Student Group Says School Segregated, Lacks Key Classes." *Denver Post.* August 9, 2002.

Krugman, Paul. "Don't Blame Bush." *New York. Times.* May 18, 2007.

Krugman, Paul. "The Waiting Game." *New York. Times.* July 16, 2007.

Kumar, Ruma. "Charter School Closure Is Certain." *Baltimore Sun.* July 12, 2007, Local: 2B.

Kuttner, Robert. "President Bush's Proposed Ownership Society Invites a History Lesson: The Great American Middle Class is the Fruit of Social Investment." *American Prospect.* May 5, 2005.

Labaton, Stephen. "Microsoft Finds Legal Defender in Justice Department." *New York Times.* June 10, 2007.

Lewin, Kurt. "Defining the Field at a Given Time." *Psychological Review.* 50 (1943), pp. 292–310. Republished in *Resolving Social Conflicts & Field Theory in Social Science.* (Washington, DC: American Psychological Association, 1997).

Lips, Dan. "Reagan's ABCs." *National Review.* March 22, 2001 (July 30, 2007).

Martin, R. Eden. "It's Too Easy for Illinois Teachers to Strike." *Chicago Sun-Times.* May 30, 2007.

Meier, Deborah, *In Schools We Trust: Creating Communities of Learning in an Era of Testing and Standardization.* (Boston, MA: Beacon Press, 2002).

Meier, Deborah and George Wood, *Many Children Left Behind: How The No Child Left Behind Act is Damaging Our Children and Our Schools. (*Boston, MA: Beacon Press, 2004).

Metcalf, Stephen. "Reading Between The Lines." *The Nation.* January 28, 2002.

Miner, Barbara. "Privatization: Rip-Offs and Resistance." *Multinational Monitor*. January 1, 2002.

Miron, Gary. "Evaluation of the Delaware Charter School Reform: Year 1 Report." 2004, The Evaluation Center, Western Michigan University.

Molnar, Alex, David R. Garcia, Gary Miron, and Shannon Berry. *Profiles Of For-profit Education Management Organizations: 2005–2006*. (Tempe, AZ: Commercialism in Education Research Unit. Arizona State University, 2005).

Moore, Stephen. *Bullish on Bush: How George W. Bush's Ownership Society Will Make America Stronger*. (New York: Derrydale, 2004).

Moyers, Bill. "For America's Sake." *The Nation*. January 2007 (July 2, 2007).

Murray, Brendan. "Bush's 'Ownership Society' Founders as U.S. Economy Weakens." Bloomberg.com. March 21, 2007.

Nakumura, David. "Big-name Consultants Greeted With Wariness." *Washington Post*. June 24, 2007, p. C06.

Nathan, Joe. *Charter Schools: Creating Hope and Opportunity for American Education*, The Jossey-Bass Education Series. (San Francisco, CA: Jossey-Bass, 1998).

National Center on Education and the Economy. *Tough Choices or Tough Times: The Report of the New Commission on the Skills of the American Workforce*. (San Francisco, CA: Jossey-Bass, 2006).

National Commission of Excellence in Education. *A Nation at Risk: The Imperative for Educational Reform*. (Washington, DC: U.S. Government Printing Office, 1983).

New York Times. "Exploding the Charter School Myth." Editorial. August 27, 2006.

Paige, Rod. *The War Against Hope: How Teachers' Unions Hurt Children, Hinder Teachers, and Endanger Public Education*. (Nashville, TN: Thomas Nelson, 2006).

Paulson, Michael. "Gingrich Drives Hard on Behalf of Microsoft." *Seattle Post-Intelligencer*. August 26, 1998.

Payne, Charles. "More Than a Symbol of Freedom: Education for Liberation and Democracy." *Phi Delta Kappan*. Vol. 85, No. 1 (September 2003), pp. 22–8.

Petrilli, Michael. "Why Not Catholic Charter Schools?" *The Education Gadfly*. December 6, 2007. http://www.edexcellence.net/foundation/gadfly/index.cfm#3732.

Reich, Robert B. "What Ownership Society?" Tompaine.Common Sense. September 2, 2004.

Richmond, Greg. "Piecing Together The Charter Puzzle." *Education Week.* Vol. 26, No. 33 (2007), pp. 28–9.

Robelen, Eric W. "Venture Fund Fueling Push for New Schools." *Education Week.* Vol. 20, No. 39 (2007), pp. 25–9.

Rotherham, Andrew. "Sorry Schools: Unions Aren't The Only Problem." *New York Post.* March 11, 2007 (July 30, 2007).

Sager, Ryan. "The Ownership Society and its Discontents." *Reason.* Vol. 38, No. 6, (2006), pp. 42–50.

Saloma, John. *Ominous Politics: The New Conservative Labyrinth.* (New York: Hill & Wang, 1984).

Saltman, Kenneth. *Schooling and the Politics of Disaster.* (New York: Routledge, 2007).

Sarason, Seymour. *Revisiting "The Culture of the School and the Problem of Change."* (New York: Teachers College Press: 1996).

Sautter, R. Craig. *Charter Schools: A New Breed Of Public Schools (Policy Briefs/North Central Regional Educational Laboratory).* (Oak Brook, IL: North Central Regional Educational Laboratory, 1995).

Scherer, Michael. "Some of Bush's Largest Donors Stand to Profit From Privatizing Public Education." *Mother Jones.* March 5, 2001.

Shipps, Dorothy. *School Reform, Corporate Style: Chicago, 1880–2000.* Studies in Government and Public Policy. (Lawrence, KS: University Press of Kansas, 2006).

Sizer, Ted. *Horace's Compromise: The Dilemma of the American High School.* (New York: Houghton Mifflin, 1984).

Sizer, Ted. *Horace's School: Redesigning the American High School.* (New York: Houghton Mifflin, 1992).

Sizer, Ted. *Horace's Hope: What Works for the American High School.* (New York: Houghton Mifflin, 1997).

Smith, Janet and David Stovall. "Urban Geographies, Racial Inequalities, and Policymaking: World Cities as Contexts for Black Education." Paper delivered at American Educational Research Association Conference, Chicago, 2007.

Socolar, Paul. "Edison Gets $1.6 M For Students It Doesn't Have." *Philadelphia Public School Notebook.* April 1, 2007. http://www.thenotebook.org/editions/2007/spring/edison.htm.

Stark, Mallory. "Lessons From Privately Managed Schools." *Harvard Business School,* 1 (2005) (June 2, 2007).

Stepp, Diane. "Charter School Companies Eyeing Georgia." *Atlanta Journal-Constitution.* April 24, 2007.

Steptoe, Sonja and Claudia Wallis. "How to Bring Our Schools Out of the 20th Century." *Time*. December 10, 2006.

Stone, C. "Civic Capacity and Urban Education." *Urban Affairs Review*. Vol. 36, No. 5 (2001), pp. 595–619.

Sweet, Kim "Small Schools, Few Choices: How New York City's High School Reform Effort Left Students With Disabilities Behind." *Parents for Inclusive Education*. October 1, 2006.

Tucker, Marc. "Making Tough Choices." *Phi Delta Kappan*. Vol. 88. No. 10 (June 2007).

Washington Post. "Can D.C. Schools Be Fixed?" Editorial. June 10, 2007.

Wasley, Patricia, Linda C. Powell, Esther Mosak, Sherry P. King, Nicole E. Holland, Matt Gladden and Michelle Fine. *Small Schools: Great Strides – A Study of New Small Schools in Chicago*. (New York: Bank Street College of Education, 2002).

Whittle, Christopher. *Crash Course*. (New York: Riverhead, 2005).

Yeager, Holly. "Concern Over Scrutiny of Do-it-All Philanthropists." *Financial Times*. July 5, 2006.

Zuckerbrod, Nancy. "2300 Schools: No Child Overhaul." *Time Magazine*. January 20, 2007.

Index